HUMAN CAPITAL, TECHNOLOGY, AND THE ROLE OF THE UNITED STATES IN INTERNATIONAL TRADE

JOHN F. MORRALL III

Human Capital, Technology, and the Role of the United States in International Trade

John F. Morrall III

University of Florida Press / Gainesville / 1972

Library of Congress Cataloging in Publication Data

Morrall, John F
    Human capital, technology, and the role of the United States in international trade.
    (University of Florida social sciences monograph no. 46)
    Includes bibliographical references.
    1. Commerce. 2. United States—Manufactures. 3. United States—Commerce. I. Title. II. Series: Florida. University, Gainesville. University of Florida monographs. Social sciences, no. 46.
HF1007.M59   382'.0973   72-2176
ISBN 0-8130-0358-X (pbk.)

SERIES DESIGNED BY STANLEY D. HARRIS

PRINTED BY THE
STORTER PRINTING COMPANY
GAINESVILLE, FLORIDA

Preface

At the present time there are two major interpretations of the observed patterns of United States foreign trade in manufactures. Both lines of thought trace their antecedents far back in the history of economic thought, although one has always occupied the mainstream while the other has always lapped at the fringes. Indeed, the latter theory has arisen mainly as a reaction to the conventional theory and consisted, until recently, of an unorganized body of criticism rather than an integrated, self-contained theory. In this study I will examine the two theories, attempting to reconcile their differences and solidify their similarities. This course of action was chosen because I felt that the two theories were complementary on theoretical grounds. However, as an explanation for United States trade, this conciliatory approach did not prove fruitful, because one theory did prove to be superior to the other by several methods of determination.

I would like to thank Professor Dennis Appleyard for his much needed criticism of several drafts of this monograph as well as for providing most of the inspiration and direction of the project. Professors Alfred Field and George Iden also read and commented on an earlier draft of the manuscript and their help is gratefully acknowledged.

The University of North Carolina at Chapel Hill and the University of Florida both provided financial support, without which this project could not have been accomplished.

By dedicating this monograph to my wife, Anne, I thank her for typing, editing, and moral support.

Thanks must go also to the Graduate School of the University of Florida for making possible the publication of this monograph.

Contents

1. The Human Capital Approach to International Trade Theory

THE ANTECEDENTS of the traditional Heckscher-Ohlin theory can be separated into three distinct approaches:[1] (1) classical comparative cost theory developed by Ricardo; (2) opportunity cost theory developed by Haberler; and (3) the factor proportions theory developed by Heckscher and Ohlin. Richard Caves has pointed out that Haberler's analysis and the Heckscher-Ohlin model are by no means in conflict. Indeed, he concludes that the former is "basically a condensed presentation" of the latter.[2] Furthermore, the classical comparative costs theory is not necessarily in conflict with factor endowment theory, since the latter seeks to explore the basis for comparative advantage while the former simply assumes that a basis exists. That the two approaches have been in conflict is due to the differing results that were uncovered when empirical verification was attempted.[3]

1. M. O. Clement, Richard L. Pfister, and Kenneth J. Rothwell, *Theoretical Issues in International Economics* (Boston: Houghton-Mifflin Company, 1967), pp. 82–85.

2. *Trade and Economic Structure: Models and Methods* (Cambridge: Harvard University Press, 1960), p. 30.

3. For example, see Bela Balassa, "An Empirical Demonstration of Classical Comparative Cost Theory," *Review of Economics and Statistics* 45 (August 1963): 231–38; Wassily W. Leontief, "Domestic Production and Foreign Trade; The American Capital Position Re-examined," *Economia Internazionale* 7 (February 1954): 3–32, reprinted in *Readings in International Economics*, eds. Richard E. Caves and Harry G. Johnson (Homewood, Illinois: Richard D. Irwin, Inc., 1968), pp. 503–27; Leontief, "Factor Proportions and the Structure of American Trade: Further Theoretical and Empirical Analysis," *Review of Economics and Statistics* 38 (November 1956): 386–407; and G. D. A. MacDougall, "British and American Exports: A Study Suggested by the Theory of Comparative Costs," *Economic Journal* 41 (December 1951): 697–724. The Balassa and MacDougall studies strongly support the comparative cost theory while the Leontief studies show results in opposition to those predicted a priori by the Heckscher-Ohlin theory, giving rise to the famous Leontief Paradox.

1

Until human capital and natural resources were added as factors of production to the Heckscher-Ohlin model, the weight of empirical evidence was overwhelmingly on the side of classical comparative advantage. Indeed, Caves thought that the classical theory would eventually win out because of its superior statistical support (p. 281). When the study is restricted to trade in manufactures so that direct trade in natural resources, which are notoriously capital intensive, is excluded,[4] and when labor skills or human capital is explicitly taken into account, the famous Leontief Paradox seems to disappear.

Leontief himself was the first to realize this. In attempting to resolve his surprising finding that the United States, seemingly capital abundant, augmented through trade its relatively abundant factor of production rather than its scarce factor, as the Heckscher-Ohlin theory predicts, Leontief deduced that American labor was three times more productive than foreign labor.[5] And, in his later article, he showed that United States exports, relative to import substitutes, were skill intensive when the labor component was broken down into five skill categories.[6] Peter Kenen then took the concept of human capital as developed by Theodore Schultz and Gary Becker[7] and capitalized the earnings differentials between unskilled laborers and Leontief's five skill categories; he then added the resulting human capital estimates to the tangible capital estimates that Leontief had derived for 1947 United States exports and competitive imports. His results tended to reverse factor intensities. At a 9 per cent capitalization rate, United States exports are total capital intensive, while United States competitive imports are labor intensive.[8] Actually, his procedure barely reverses the factor intensities,

---

4. See Jaroslav Vanek, *The Natural Resource Content of United States Foreign Trade, 1870–1955* (Cambridge: M.I.T. Press, 1963), pp. 128–35. Vanek finds a "strong degree of complementarity between capital and natural resource requirements" and this, combined with his major finding that the United States has experienced an increasing scarcity of natural resources which it has tried to augment through foreign trade, leads him to conclude that the Leontief Paradox could be explained by the combination of these two factors.

5. "Domestic Production and Foreign Trade," p. 525.

6. "Factor Proportions and the Structure of American Trade," p. 399.

7. See Schultz, "Reflections on Investment in Man," *Journal of Political Economy* 70 Supplement (October 1962): 1–8; and Becker, "Investment in Human Capital," ibid., pp. 9–49; and Becker, *Human Capital* (New York: National Bureau of Economic Research, 1964).

8. Peter B. Kenen, "Nature, Capital, and Trade," *Journal of Political Economy* 73 (October 1965): 456–58.

and at a 12.7 per cent capitalization rate it fails to dispel the Leontief Paradox.[9]

Donald Keesing, in a series of important articles, proceeded more directly along the lines suggested by Leontief by refining the concept of labor skills.[10] He does not attempt to give a dollar estimate of human capital, but instead alters the Heckscher-Ohlin model by identifying four major factors of production: natural resources, physical capital, and skilled and unskilled labor. He also points out that by concentrating on manufactures we can eliminate natural resources, and that, inasmuch as capital moves internationally at a much lower cost than does labor, the general skills possessed by an economy are apt to change much more slowly than its physical capital structure.[11] This will be especially true if skilled workers are needed to train more skilled workers of the same type.[12] Keesing establishes a strong case for the prolonged influence of slowly changing relative skill endowments on trade patterns in manufactures. He has classified skill levels far more specifically than Leontief did, and, for the first time, scientists and engineers have been introduced as a separate—and the most skill intensive—category. In analyzing the skill requirements needed to produce United States exports and imports for 1962, Keesing found that the higher the skill level, the greater the difference in skill requirements. To produce United

9. Evidence from another country, however, supports Kenen's emphasis on human capital. Karl W. Roskamp, in "Factor Proportions and Foreign Trade: The Case of West Germany," *Weltwirtschaftliches Archiv* 2 (1963): 319–26, found (consistent with the Leontief Paradox) that German exports in 1954 were capital intensive relative to the United States. However, Roskamp and Gordon C. McMeekin, in "Factor Proportions, Human Capital and Foreign Trade: The Case of West Germany Reconsidered," *Quarterly Journal of Economics* 82 (February 1968): 152–60, again using a 55-sector input-output table for 1954 West Germany, but this time introducing human capital as a third factor of production, found, as one would expect a priori, that human capital was the relatively most abundant factor and physical capital the relatively least abundant, with unskilled labor occupying the intermediate position. The second article reverses the Leontief Paradox.

10. "Labor Skills and International Trade: Evaluating Many Trade Flows with a Single Measuring Device," *Review of Economics and Statistics* 47 (August 1965): 287–94; "Labor Skills and Comparative Advantage," *American Economic Review Proceedings* 56 (May 1966): 249–54; and "Labor Skills and the Structure of Trade in Manufactures," in *The Open Economy: Essays on International Trade and Finance*, eds. P. B. Kenen and R. Lawrence, Columbia Studies in Economics, vol. 1 (New York: Columbia University Press, 1968), pp. 3–18.

11. "Labor Skills and the Structure of Trade in Manufactures," p. 6.

12. "Labor Skills and Comparative Advantage," p. 252.

States exports, it was necessary that 5.02 per cent (34,430) of the labor force consist of scientists and engineers, while for the United States to produce its imports, only 2.77 per cent (9,762 scientists and engineers) would have been required. In correlating skill requirements with a measure of export performance, the percentage of United States exports to fourteen industrial nations' total exports, Keesing found that scientists and engineers as a percentage of the labor force in thirty-five manufacturing industries explained 50 per cent of the variation. This was by far the highest R^2 for any skill class with unskilled labor following with a negative correlation coefficient of −64. Thus, Keesing concluded "that United States comparative advantage centers in industries involving a high percentage of professional labor and a low percentage of unskilled labor."[13]

David Ball also found that United States 1960 exports were skill intensive for twenty manufacturing industries, this pattern being consistent along Heckscher-Ohlin lines with the assumption that the United States was both tangible capital and human capital abundant compared with the rest of the world.[14] He also found that the United States' scarce factor, unskilled labor, is protected by higher effective tariff rates than our abundant factor, skilled labor.[15] This is as the Heckscher-Ohlin theory predicts. The scarce factor of production is apt to suffer from free trade because the scarce factor is augmented through imports, while demand for the abundant factor, embodied in exports, is increased.[16]

Helen Waehrer has investigated Irving Kravis' findings[17] that United States export industries are characterized by higher average

13. Ibid., pp. 255–58.

14. "Studies in the Basis of International Trade" (Ph.D. diss., University of North Carolina, 1967), chap. 6.

15. Ibid., chap. 5. Also see Ball, "U.S. Effective Tariffs and Labor's Share," *Journal of Political Economy* 75 (April 1967): 183–87. William Travis has also provided extensive support for the contention that the scarce factor seeks to limit the volume of trade through protection. However, his model is the traditional capital and labor model without human capital. His study is further weakened by his use of nominal tariffs rather than effective tariffs (see *The Theory of Trade and Protection* [Cambridge: Harvard University Press, 1964]).

16. See Wolfgang F. Stolper and Paul A. Samuelson, "Protection and Real Wages," *Review of Economic Studies* 9 (November 1941): 58–73, reprinted in *Readings in the Theory of International Trade,* eds. Howard S. Ellis and Lloyd A. Metzler (Homewood, Illinois: Richard D. Irwin, Inc., 1950), pp. 333–57.

17. "Wages and Foreign Trade," *Review of Economics and Statistics* 34 (February 1956): 14–30.

wages than United States import-competing industries, a finding that is not predicted by, although neither is it necessarily inconsistent with, either classical comparative advantage or unmodified Heckscher-Ohlin theory. Both theories predict that the structure of trade should be determined by inter-industry differences in factor productivities (the former theory simply assuming them and the latter explaining them by factor proportions). Waehrer's explanation, and one also mentioned by Ball, is that high wages are associated with human capital or labor skills as predicted by Schultz and Becker and that the United States' comparative advantage is associated with a relatively abundant factor of production, skilled labor, a claim made by Leontief and Keesing.[18] Indeed, Waehrer's statistical results confirm her hypothesis. Using thirty-five industries, the correlation coefficient between an index of trade performance and a skill index was greater than the correlation coefficient between trade performance and the average wage rate.[19] The high wages and high productivity of net export industries found in many studies can be explained by their relative human capital intensity.[20]

The empirical conflict between the Heckscher-Ohlin model and classical comparative advantage, one that Caves and others[21]

18. Helen Waehrer, "Wage Rates, Labor Skills, and United States Foreign Trade," in Kenen and Lawrence, *The Open Economy*, p. 25; Ball, "Studies in the Basis of International Trade," p. 142.

19. Waehrer, p. 37. The correlation coefficient was $+.50$ between the skill index and the net trade balance vs. $+.43$ for annual wages and the trade index.

20. In addition to the Kravis and Waehrer studies, MacDougall and Balassa also found higher relative productivities in export industries.

21. Note the views of the leading textbook writers in the field. Charles P. Kindleberger, in *Foreign Trade and the National Economy* (New Haven: Yale University Press, 1962), p. 75, states that "What he [Leontief] proves is not that the United States is capital-scarce and labor-abundant, but that the Heckscher-Ohlin theorem is wrong." And Ingo Walter, in *International Economics: Theory and Policy* (New York: Ronald Press Company, 1968), p. 136, concludes: "The classical theory of comparative costs based on differences in productivity levels emerges as an important determinant of trade patterns, judging from the empirical studies surveyed. Experience with the factor-endowments model seems to show a somewhat more limited predictive value, although numerous and complex considerations are involved which, if taken into account, might change the picture quite materially." As pointed out above, these two theories are not necessarily in conflict, since the classical comparative advantage theory stops short of explaining why factor productivities differ. The Heckscher-Ohlin theory goes on to attribute the differing factor productivities to differing factor proportions. Therefore, a rejection of the Heckscher-Ohlin theory actually weakens the more general classical comparative advantage theory in the sense that the differing factor productivities must now be explained by influences other than factor proportions.

thought was being resolved in favor of classical comparative advantage, seems to disappear when the Heckscher-Ohlin model is extended to more than two factors of production, as indeed Heckscher and Ohlin had originally intended.[22] If there is any validity to the assumption that unskilled labor is a relatively scarce factor in the United States, then the prediction of the factor proportions theory, that United States exports will be skill intensive and imports unskilled intensive, is borne out for United States trade data for the years 1947, 1957, 1960, and 1962. The Leontief Paradox disappears.

The empirical studies by MacDougall, Balassa, and Kravis in support of the classical comparative advantage theory are thus no longer in conflict with the modified Heckscher-Ohlin approach, since relatively greater skill intensities may explain the relatively greater labor productivity observed in United States export industries, compared with import-competing industries.[23] When it was found that a higher ratio of physical capital to labor was not the cause of the greater productivity of labor in United States export industries, attention was diverted from a factor proportions explanation of productivity differences to one of differing technologies. This, of course, violates the Heckscher-Ohlin assumption of similar production functions for identical goods produced in different countries. However, the labor-skills approach reduces the need to turn to theories that violate the assumptions of the Heckscher-Ohlin theory, although it does not vitiate the fact that explanations such as differing technologies can explain a large portion of trade in manufactures.

The introduction of labor skills or human capital as well as natural resources as explicit factors of production also blunts the force of another kind of attack on the Heckscher-Ohlin model. The model has been criticized because of the possibility that factor intensity reversals could occur which would destroy its operational significance since it would no longer be possible to identify different industries as to their factor intensities. A factor intensity reversal occurs when a factor of production changes to the unintensive

22. See Eli Heckscher, "The Effect of Foreign Trade on the Distribution of Income," *Ekonomisk Tidskrift* 21 (1919): 497–512, reprinted in Ellis and Metzler, *Readings*, p. 279.

23. For an in-depth investigation of this proposition see Ball, "Studies in the Basis of International Trade," chap. 7.

rather than the intensive factor in the production of one good relative to another good. With a given production function, this can occur among countries when relative factor prices differ to a sufficient degree, or, with given prices, it can occur if production functions for a given industry differ to a sufficient degree from country to country (i.e., they use different technologies, which, of course, is a violation of the Heckscher-Ohlin assumptions). The importance of this phenomenon to international trade theory is essentially an empirical question and probably would not have arisen if it had not been for the soul-searching brought about by the Leontief Paradox and its aftermath.[24]

Empirical investigation was instigated by one group along two lines. Arrow, Chenery, Minhas, and Solow, and later Minhas alone, in developing their "constant elasticity of substitution" production function, estimated the elasticities for physical capital/labor substitution for various industries by using international data.[25] Using a CES production function, rather than the Cobb-Douglas production function, allows elasticities to vary among industries; if they do vary, then as relative factor prices change, some industries will undergo factor intensity reversals faster than others. Minhas then identifies possible factor intensity reversals within the actual Asian–United States relative factor price range (p. 38). He also uses a more general test, one that does not depend on the artificial assumption of constant elasticities. He simply ranks twenty industries by capital intensity for the United States and Japan, using both value added and total capital estimates (p. 40). The dissimilarity in the rankings leads him to reject the strong factor intensity hypothesis (i.e., no reversals) and the empirical relevance of the Heckscher-Ohlin theory in predicting the direction of trade (p. 50).

But here also the explicit addition of natural resources and human capital to the Heckscher-Ohlin model serves to dispel doubts about the strong factor intensity hypothesis. It also provides indirect

24. Before Leontief's result had been made known, Paul A. Samuelson, in "A Comment on Factor Price Equalization," *Review of Economic Studies* 29 (1951–52): 121–22, observed that "the phenomenon of goods that interchange their roles of being labor intensive is much less important empirically than it is interesting theoretically."

25. See K. Arrow, H. B. Chenery, B. S. Minhas, and R. M. Solow, "Capital-labor Substitution and Economic Efficiency," *Review of Economics and Statistics* 43 (August 1961): 225–50; and B. S. Minhas, *An International Comparison of Factor Costs and Factor Use* (Amsterdam: North Holland, 1963).

evidence that technologies are the same among nations because factor intensity reversals would be expected to occur if they differed. Ball and Hufbauer, at about the same time, criticized Minhas for the inclusion of certain industries in his analysis of United States and Japanese capital intensities.[26] Ball argued that the natural resource based industries of agriculture, and, to a lesser extent, grain mill products and processed foods should not be included due to the dissimilarity in composition of output, the influence of natural resources, the differing diffusion rates of technology, and the less reliable statistics in the agricultural sectors of the two countries. Removing agriculture from the rankings of direct capital intensity raises the Spearman rank correlation from +.733 to +.833, and removing the three food-related industries from the total physical capital intensity rankings raises the Spearman coefficient from +.339 to +.765; in both cases the probability is less than 1 per cent that these rankings could have occurred by chance.[27]

These results were attained before recognition was made of the fourth factor of production. When allowance is made for different endowments in labor skills, the case against factor reversals is even stronger. Specifically, with regard to Minhas' estimates of the elasticities of substitution for different industries, Kenen has shown, theoretically, and Merle Yahr, empirically,[28] that the inclusion of human capital systematically biases the elasticity estimates. Yahr has estimated CES production functions for nineteen industries and twenty countries with human capital held constant and concluded that "there are no statistically significant differences among elasticities of substitution," and, therefore, "these empirical results substantiate the strong factor-intensity assumption" (p. 90). She finds that the systematic bias that occurs when human capital is not recognized is one of labor substitution by the countries that are more human capital abundant (p. 98). This is empirical evidence for Ball's tentative suggestion that a higher relative use of skilled labor in devel-

26. See Ball, "Studies in the Basis of International Trade," chap. 2, and his "Factor Intensity Reversals in International Comparison of Factor Costs and Factor Use," *Journal of Political Economy* (February 1966): 77–80, based on this chapter; and Gary Hufbauer, *Synthetic Materials and the Theory of International Trade* (Cambridge: Harvard University Press, 1966), Appendix B, pp. 113–20.

27. "Studies in the Basis of International Trade," pp. 30–33.

28. Kenen, "Nature, Capital, and Trade," p. 456; Yahr, "Human Capital and Factor Substitution in the CES Production Function," in *The Open Economy*, pp. 70–99.

oped countries compared to underdeveloped countries might explain why Victor Fuchs' elasticity of capital-labor substitution estimates, using the same countries that Yahr and Minhas worked with, turned out to be "typically about one" when a dummy variable was used to separate developed from underdeveloped countries.[29] Fuchs' own explanation was that fringe benefits might be a greater percentage of labor costs in underdeveloped countries than in developed countries, but he presents no empirical evidence that this is so.[30] Either explanation serves to weaken the empirical validity of Minhas' factor reversal argument.

Finally, Hal Lary of the National Bureau of Economic Research has tested extensively for factor intensity reversals using measures of direct total capital intensity (value added per employee), direct human capital intensity (wage value added per employee), and direct physical capital (non-wage value added per employee).[31] He examines the extent of factor reversals in the following groups: 3 industry groups and 20 countries, 13 industry groups and 9 countries, the United States and the United Kingdom for 103 industries, the United States and Japan for 178 industries, and the United States and India for 117 industries. He concludes: "To sum up, the international comparisons made in this chapter tend to support the general validity of the strong-factor-intensity hypothesis and, more particularly, the relevance of the United States pattern of factor intensities to other countries at very different levels of development and with very different factor-price ratios" (p. 80).

29. Ball, "Studies in the Basis of International Trade," pp. 63–70. Ball is commenting on Victor R. Fuchs, "Capital-Labor Substitution: A Note," *Review of Economics and Statistics* 45 (November 1963): 436–38. The tendency for a unitary elasticity in most of the industries once the dummy variable is introduced implies that factor-intensity reversals take place mainly between developed and underdeveloped countries. Minhas' results depend on the existence of two populations of countries. One of the main differences between the two populations is the abundance of human capital.

30. Pages 437–38. See Harold Lydall, *The Structure of Earnings* (London: Oxford University Press, 1968), pp. 44–45, for the opposite view that fringe benefits are of more importance in richer nations.

31. *Imports of Manufactures from Less Developed Countries,* Studies in International Economic Relations, 4 (New York: National Bureau of Economic Research, 1968), chap. 3. Lary goes to some length in appendices to show that his measures of human and physical capital are good proxies for the conventional, more direct estimates. Lary also justifies the use of value added data which measure only direct inputs (thus differing from Leontief's input-output approach) on grounds of availability of data and the fact that intermediate products are "ubiquitous or readily transportable" (p. 15).

The combined weight of the above evidence tends to support the factor proportions approach in two ways. The former empirical conflicts found in testing the two theories have been eliminated, while the alternative to the Heckscher-Ohlin explanation for differing factor productivities (i.e., differing technologies) has been found to be unimportant due to the lack of large-scale factor intensity reversals in broad industry groups when natural resources and human capital are included in the analysis. This last point needs more elaboration. Given that the strong factor assumption holds, then in order for technologies to differ among the industries of different countries, the technologies must be neutrally different, not biased toward either labor or capital saving. If productivities of different industries differed in a more complicated fashion than a multiplicative constant, including one, then factor intensity reversals would be expected to occur. Thus, the evidence that supports the findings that factor intensity reversals are empirically unimportant also rules out a large class of differing technology explanations of trade patterns.

Lary attempts to make some predictions and recommendations from his array of relative human and physical capital intensity rankings for seventy-seven United States industries with regard to the products that the less developed countries should now, or will in the future, be exporting to the developed countries (pp. 23–30). Since less developed countries are characterized by a lack of both physical and human capital, their comparative advantage should lie in industries which require relatively less human as well as physical capital. Lary does not test these hypotheses, but instead simply lists the relatively unskilled labor intensive industries in the United States that, at the Standard International Trade Classification three-digit level, have imports by the developed from the underdeveloped nations of at least $100,000.[32] As a guide to future policy for the underdeveloped countries, this ex post procedure is rather mute.

Although the studies cited earlier support Lary's belief that his list has predictive power, his methods should be subjected to empirical verification. Therefore, it is revealing to compare his esti-

32. Pages 86–90. Lary defines as labor intensive all industries in the United States that have value added per employee that does not exceed the national average for all manufacturing in the United States by more than 10 per cent.

mates for 1965 human, physical, and total capital intensity of United States manufactures with 1965 United States net exports at the two-digit level. If Lary is going to use United States factor intensities to predict industries in which the developing countries have a comparative advantage, this procedure should certainly be able to predict industries in which the United States' comparative advantage lies.

Table 1 lists the twenty United States industries at the two-digit level along with their 1965 net exports, and net exports as a percentage of total shipments computed by the writer from the *1964 and 1965 Annual Survey of Manufactures* and from Lary's estimates of 1965 total, physical, and human capital in these industries. Table 3 presents a summary of Spearman rank coefficients. What is most surprising are the low values of the coefficients for 1965 net exports and value added per employee, and 1965 net exports and wage value added per employee, +.292, and +.347, respectively. These coefficients are not even significant at the .05 level. However, these variables correlated with net exports as a percentage of value of shipments do produce coefficients of +.523, and +.487, which are significant at the .05 level but not at the .01 level. Lary seems to be claiming more than his procedures justify. These results, though, are surprising because for 1960, both Ball, using the same twenty industries, and Waehrer, using a thirty-five-industry sample, achieved much better results.[33] Ball's data for 1960 are reproduced in Table 2, and the Spearman coefficients he computed are shown in Table 3. Ball calculated Spearman correlation coefficients of +.723 between net exports and value added per employee, and +.735 between net exports and wage value added per employee, both significant at the .01 level. The reason for the wide difference in results for the two years is not a change in factor intensities, because the Spearman coefficients between 1960 and 1965 value added per employee and wage value added per employee were found to be +.965, and +.974, respectively.

The main reason why Ball's 1960 results support the Heckscher-Ohlin theory much more strongly than our 1965 results appears to be a difference in the data defined as "competitive imports," which are subtracted from exports to get the measure of export perform-

33. Waehrer, pp. 43–46. For the thirty-five industries, Waehrer computed a correlation coefficient of +.43, significant at the .01 level, between annual wage and net export balance. Ball's results are reproduced in the text.

TABLE 1.—1965 TRADE AND FACTOR INTENSITY CHARACTERISTICS OF U.S. MANUFACTURING INDUSTRIES

SIC NUMBER AND INDUSTRY	NET EXPORTS[a] (millions)	NET EXPORTS AS % OF SHIPMENTS[b]	INDEX OF VALUE ADDED PER EMPLOYEE		
			Total[e]	Wages and salaries[e]	Other[e]
20 Food and kindred products	$80	.1%	109	91	124
21 Tobacco products	118	2.5	84	77	123
22 Textile mill products	-473	-2.6	64	72	57
23 Apparel and related products	-364	-2.0	49	61	39
24 Lumber and wood products	-408	-4.0	59	73	46
25 Furniture and fixtures	-17	-.3	68	81	56
26 Paper and allied products	-658	-3.6	105	104	107
27 Printing and publishing	153	.8	94	104	85
28 Chemicals and allied products	1,960	5.3	193	126	303
29 Petroleum and coal products	-486	-2.6	220	126	303
30 Rubber and plastic products	74	.7	93	99	88
31 Leather and leather products	-196	-4.2	53	66	42
32 Stone, clay, and glass products	15	.1	101	97	104
33 Primary metal industries	-1,341	-3.0	115	121	110
34 Fabricated metal products	541	2.0	93	103	84
35 Machinery except electrical	4,015	10.2	105	116	95
36 Electrical machinery	765	2.2	96	105	88
37 Transportation equipment	2,010	3.0	122	128	116
38 Instruments and related products	408	5.4	117	110	124
39 Miscellaneous manufacturing	-239	-3.2	81	81	82

[a]Calculated by subtracting competitive imports from exports as found in the U.S. Bureau of the Census, *U.S. Commodity Exports and Imports as Related to Output, 1966 and 1965* (Washington, 1968), Table 1c, pp. 24–57.

[b]Net exports divided by shipments as found in U.S. Bureau of the Census, *Annual Survey of Manufactures: 1964 and 1965* (Washington, 1968), Table 2, p. 14.

[e]From Lary, *Imports of Manufactures from Less Developed Countries*, Table 2, pp. 24–29.

TABLE 2.—1960 TRADE AND FACTOR INTENSITY CHARACTERISTICS OF U.S. MANUFACTURING INDUSTRIES

SIC NUMBER AND INDUSTRY	NET EXPORTS[a] (millions)	AVERAGE ANNUAL WAGE ALL EMPLOYEES[a]	VALUE ADDED PER WORKER[a]
20 Food and kindred products	$1,158.5	$4,779	$11,478
21 Tobacco products	421.3	3,871	18,727
22 Textile mill products	−361.3	3,567	6,305
23 Apparel and related products	−208.5	3,130	5,329
24 Lumber and wood products	− 27.0	3,639	6,849
25 Furniture and fixtures	8.2	4,196	7,182
26 Paper and allied products	307.2	5,378	11,320
27 Printing and publishing	94.5	5,576	10,197
28 Chemicals and allied products	1,362.4	6,119	19,905
29 Petroleum and coal products	458.2	6,693	19,018
30 Rubber and plastic products	106.5	5,285	9,978
31 Leather and leather products	− 54.9	3,431	5,713
32 Stone, clay, and glass products	− 70.5	5,055	10,777
33 Primary metal industries	519.4	6,136	11,298
34 Fabricated metal products	264.3	5,149	9,477
35 Machinery except electrical	2,542.0	5,930	10,095
36 Electrical machinery	622.4	5,391	9,750
37 Transportation equipment	1,808.9	6,512	11,547
38 Instruments and related products	182.0	5,919	11,272
39 Miscellaneous manufacturing	74.1	5,333	8,976

[a]From Ball, "Studies in the Basis of International Trade," Table 15, pp. 115–16. Ball's net export figures are derived from a different source than the net export figures in Table 1. See pp. 11, 15 for further explanation.

TABLE 3.—SUMMARY OF COEFFICIENTS OF RANK CORRELATION BETWEEN INDICES
OF TRADE COMPETITIVENESS AND FACTOR INTENSITIES

	NET EXPORTS (1965) [a]	NET EXPORTS AS % OF SHIPMENTS (1965) [a]	NET EXPORTS (1960) [b]
Twenty industries			
Value added per employee	.292	.523*	.723**
Wage value added per employee	.347	.487*	.735**
Non-wage value added per employee	.255	.483*	.583**
Eighteen industries (SIC 29 and 33 eliminated)			
Value added per employee	.633**	.739**	
Wage value added per employee	.731**	.745**	
Sixteen industries (SIC 21, 26, 29, and 33 eliminated)			
Value added per employee	.829**	.833**	.733**
Wage value added per employee	.941**	.934**	.815**

*Indicates statistical significance at the .05 level.
**Indicates statistical significance at the .01 level.
[a] 1965 correlation coefficients computed by the writer from Table 1.
[b] Correlation coefficients for twenty industries as computed by Ball, "Studies in the Basis of International Trade," Table 17, p. 134. The 1960 net exports should not be compared to the 1965 net exports. For explanation see the text.

ance, "net exports." The data Ball has used for exports and "competitive imports" are from two separate Department of Labor studies, while my data for 1965, for both exports and imports, are from a Department of Commerce publication which specifically attempts to make comparable exports, imports, and domestic output figures.[34]

The Department of Labor's publication *Employment in Relation to U.S. Imports, 1960,* used by Ball, biases the export performance index in a specific direction, because it excludes from competitive imports "(1) those raw material and semi-manufactured products which furnish more than 75 per cent, or less than 5 per cent, of the total U.S. supply, and (2) those which supply less than three-fourths of U.S. requirements and more than 5 per cent but have been judged essential to U.S. industry" (pp. 1–2). Thus, this arbitrary definition tends to eliminate many raw material based imports from the picture. A true test of the Heckscher-Ohlin model should take into account the influence of natural resources in a more open way, perhaps by including natural resources as a factor of production. To investigate the importance of natural resources, already hinted at by a comparison of my data and Ball's, this procedure was followed. Petroleum and coal products (sic 29) and the primary metal industries (sic 33) were identified as natural resource based industries and eliminated from our calculations. When this was done, Spearman coefficients shown in Table 3 between net exports and total and human capital rose to +.633 and +.731. Furthermore, when tobacco manufactures (sic 21) and paper and allied products (sic 26) are eliminated by the same criterion, the coefficients rise to a startling +.829 and +.941. The last four coefficients are significant at the .01 level of probability. The finding that natural resources are extremely influential in determining net exports even of manufactures is in accordance with Vanek's thesis.[35]

34. Ball's data come from two 1962 publications of the Bureau of Labor Statistics: export data from *Domestic Employment Attributable to U.S. Exports, 1960,* pp. 8–9, and data on "competitive imports" from *Employment in Relation to U.S. Imports, 1960,* p. 11 (see "Studies in the Basis of International Trade," pp. 113–14); U.S. Bureau of the Census, *U.S. Commodity Exports and Imports as Related to Output, 1966 and 1965* (Washington, 1968).

35. Vanek, p. 130, concludes that ". . . over the past 85 years the United States has become steadily poorer in natural resources relative to the rest of the world and more abundantly endowed with other factors of production. About the time of World War I, or a little later, the natural resources of this country became scarce as compared with the rest of the world." Thus, the influence of natural resources on United States trade patterns is becoming

It is also interesting to note that if these same four eliminations are performed for Ball's 1960 data, as is done in Table 3, the improvement in the correlation coefficient is only marginal. This is due to the fact that his trade figures have already partially allowed for the natural resource influence.

Thus, the importance of natural resources poses problems for the analysis of trade patterns even for manufactures. The human capital approach, as developed by Ball and Lary, must be used in conjunction with the natural resources explanation in predicting future trade patterns and identifying industries with possible export potential for the developing countries.

However, the problem may be more involved than simply identifying natural resource influences as additions to the simple factor intensity approach developed above. There are other industries that might be considered natural resource influenced, the elimination of which would reduce the correlations. Food and kindred products (SIC 20) and lumber and wood products (SIC 24) are two such candidates. In addition, there are other reasons for the poor competitive position of some of the industries eliminated. Adams and Dirlam have blamed the decline in the competitive position of the United States' steel industries, which is the major subgroup of SIC 33, on the oligopolistic structure of that industry, which slowed down the rate of technological innovation in the United States relative to Europe and Japan.[36] Thus, the Heckscher-Ohlin approach, when modified to take into account different labor skills and natural resource influences, does explain the United States' comparative advantage fairly well. The approach, which was initially intended by its discoverers to take into account such additional factors as labor skills and natural resources, has had to return from its brief, simple, two-factor interlude to its broader formula-

---

stronger, and must be taken into account in future trade studies. Lary's assumption that intermediate products are "ubiquitous or readily transportable" seems questionable, and, therefore, his value added approach in measuring factor content is not entirely satisfactory.

36. See Walter Adams and Joel B. Dirlam, "Big Steel, Invention, and Innovation," *Quarterly Journal of Economics* 80 (May 1966): 167–89. They also mention that another oligopolistic industry, petroleum refining, a subgroup of SIC 29, which we also eliminated, has probably followed a pattern similar to the steel industry. However, this point was challenged by Alan K. McAdams, "Big Steel, Invention, and Innovation, Reconsidered," *Quarterly Journal of Economics* 81 (August 1967): 457–74, and defended by Adams and Dirlam, "Reply," ibid., pp. 475–82.

tion in order to earn empirical support. However, it appears that only four factors, tangible capital, human capital, unskilled labor, and natural resources, are needed before respectable empirical support is attained. This formulation of the Heckscher-Ohlin model will be further tested in chapter 3, but first another possibly competing explanation of international trade patterns will be examined. This new theory, the product cycle theory, has also generated considerable empirical support, and, indeed, Keesing, a pioneer in the labor skills approach, has recently moved tentatively toward this new theory.[37]

37. See "The Impact of Research and Development on United States Trade," *Journal of Political Economy* 75 (February 1967): 38–48.

2. The Product Cycle Approach to International Trade Theory

Just as the Heckscher-Ohlin theory was being reconciled, both theoretically and empirically, with classical comparative cost, a new challenger rose to confront the factor proportions explanation. Whether it is a real or illusionary challenger will now be examined.

The antecedents of product cycle theory are deep and broad, and are found mainly through the years in the criticisms of conventional trade theory. Many economists have never been entirely satisfied with conventional trade theory. Product cycle theory may be viewed as an attempt to bring into a formalized system the more telling criticisms of conventional theory. Raymond Vernon presented the first complete exposition of the product cycle theory in 1966,[1] citing five major early contributors.[2] M. V. Posner, who developed the technical gap theory of international trade, and Simon Kuznets, who first identified the product cycle in American industry, should also be cited.[3]

Summaries of the product cycle theory have been presented by Vernon and Seev Hirsch, who seem to have developed the concept together, although the two versions are quite different in content.[4]

1. "International Investment and International Trade in the Product Cycle," *Quarterly Journal of Economics* 80 (May 1966): 190–207.
2. J. H. Williams, "The Theory of International Trade Reconsidered," reprinted in his *Postwar Monetary Plans and Other Essays* (Oxford: Basil Blackwell, 1947), chap. 2; C. P. Kindleberger, *The Dollar Shortage* (New York: Wiley, 1950) (also see Kindleberger's *Foreign Trade and the National Economy*); Erik Hoffmeyer, *Dollar Shortage* (Amsterdam: North Holland, 1958); Sir Donald MacDougall, *The World Dollar Problem* (London: Macmillan, 1957); and S. B. Linder, *An Essay on Trade and Transformation* (Uppsala: Almquist & Wiksells, 1961).
3. Posner, "International Trade and Technical Change," *Oxford Economic Papers* 13 (October 1961): 323–41; Kuznets, *Economic Change* (New York: W. W. Norton & Co., 1953).
4. See Vernon, and Hirsch, *Location of Industry and International Competitiveness* (Oxford: Clarendon Press, 1967). Hirsch's book is based on his doctoral dissertation which he wrote under Vernon at the Harvard Business School in 1965.

It differs from the Heckscher-Ohlin theory in that it is explicitly dynamic, while the factor proportions theory is static. In an attempt to explain reality more fully, product cycle theory brings in far more variables than the Heckscher-Ohlin theory, and, as a result, is far less elegant. It also emphasizes the demand side more strongly than Heckscher-Ohlin, and in some versions contains the Heckscher-Ohlin theory itself as a subset. The theory as set forth by Vernon is quite different from factor proportions theory, confirming the familiar proposition that a new product (or theory) must be differentiated sufficiently from existing products so that the consumer will be induced to buy it. Thus, Vernon probably exaggerates the differences between his approach and conventional trade theory.

Briefly, Vernon starts with the idea set forth by Linder that new products will not be developed in a given country unless a market exists for them in that country.[5] The need for inexpensive communication between the producer and the market declines with geographic proximity and determines both location of innovation and early production.[6] Vernon points out that the United States' market is characterized by the highest per capita income and unit labor costs in the world, and that the new products developed in this country should, therefore, be either income elastic or labor saving. In addition, this gives us reason to expect that expenditures on research and development should be higher in the United States than in other countries, at least on products with those characteristics (p. 193). Factors related primarily to the uncertainties of producing and marketing new products, according to Vernon, are "far stronger than relative factor-cost and transportation considerations" in determining the location of the production of new products. He is rejecting not only the factor proportions theory at this point but also classical comparative cost analysis (p. 194). The characteristics of this stage of the cycle are listed by Vernon as a need for a high degree of freedom in varying inputs, a low price elasticity of demand for individual producers due to product differentiation or the existence of monopoly in the early stages, and a need for rapid and effective communication between customers and producers and the producers' suppliers and competitors. These characteristics argue for

5. Linder, pp. 88–90.
6. Vernon, p. 192. Although this is the heart of Linder's theory of trade, Vernon does not cite him except as an early contributor of "bits and pieces" of "inspiration" (p. 191).

a location of production nearer the market and call for ample and varied suppliers of potential inputs (pp. 195–96).

Over time, products become standardized, uncertainty declines, and production costs become more important. A small foreign demand for the product exists from the beginning, probably from the most wealthy individuals in other developed countries who have tastes and needs similar to the relatively well-off Americans. Eventually foreign production begins when the foreign market becomes large enough to support a plant capable of producing at an average cost lower than American marginal costs plus transportation and tariff charges. Soon price competition becomes important and the area of least cost begins to have a comparative advantage. According to Vernon, since the cost of capital, especially to international firms, is about the same in different locations, once economies of scale are reached "the principal differences between any two locations are likely to be labor costs" (p. 198). He has introduced the classical comparative cost theory into his analysis, but he is quick to retreat slightly when he points out that "any hypothesis based on the assumption that the United States entrepreneur will react rationally when offered the possibility of a lower-cost location abroad is somewhat suspect" (p. 200). Vernon seems to be claiming that cost minimization is not the motivating force driving firms to locate in low cost areas, but that it is the threatened loss of a firm's market position that provides the "powerful galvanizing force to action" (p. 200). However, any threat, if it is real, must come from a lower cost producer. Thus, he seems to be too quick in repudiating the traditional basis for comparative advantage.

Vernon also claims that his hypotheses explain the Leontief Paradox. According to the product cycle theory, the United States should be exporting products which are both high income and labor saving in their early stages and which are apt to be labor intensive, not because the labor is particularly skilled, but because large capital investments are held down due to the uncertainties associated with new products. Second, the United States should be importing products which, being in their later stages, are more standardized, and thus more physical capital intensive (pp. 201–2). Finally, he predicts that the comparative advantage of the less developed countries lies in some of the products that are at an advanced stage of standardization, although he realizes that "this is a bold projection which seems on first blush to be wholly at variance with the

Heckscher-Ohlin theorem" (p. 203). However, this projection is not at variance with the human capital modified Heckscher-Ohlin model if standardized products require little human capital and physical capital costs are about the same internationally.[7]

Although Vernon seeks to differentiate his product from the existing ones, his student, Hirsch, attempts to tie his version of the product cycle approach to a loose version of Heckscher-Ohlin theory. Hirsch relies less on Linder's theories and more on Kuznets' development of the product cycle. He is not just looking at the characteristics of the process of developing new products in the United States, but also at new products in general. He tries to identify which countries will enjoy comparative advantages at which stages of the cycle. To do this he divides the countries of the world into three categories: the developing, the advanced, and the small developed. He divides the product cycle into three stages, as does Vernon: the new, the growth, and the mature phases. He also divides the factors of production into five factors, not counting natural resources: capital, unskilled labor, management, scientific and engineering know-how, and external economies (pp. 16–41). He concludes from this framework, and from some a priori judgments concerning relative factor abundance, that the comparative advantage of the developing country lies in products that have reached their mature stage, that the advanced country's comparative advantage lies in products in their growth stage, and, finally, that the small developed country's advantage lies in new products (pp. 24–41).

Hirsch's conclusions differ from Vernon's on at least one major point. Vernon feels that new products will be developed first in, and exported by, the United States, while Hirsch maintains that the small developed countries, such as Britain, Switzerland, Holland, Sweden, and Israel, may have a comparative advantage in new products. Hirsch bases this proposition on his judgment that some small developed countries "possess engineering and scientific talents which might be obtained at comparatively lower costs." However,

7. The two theories are at variance if the Heckscher-Ohlin model is confined to the two-factor case, physical capital and labor, since standardized products are apt to be physical capital intensive while the less developed countries' relatively abundant factor is usually considered to be labor. Thus, the simple Heckscher-Ohlin model does predict the opposite from the product cycle model. However, the evidence in chapter 1 rejects the simple factor proportions model.

he realizes that the small developed countries have a comparative disadvantage in that they do not possess a relative abundance of external economies which are also important for new products.[8] Despite this realization, he still maintains that small developed countries should have a comparative advantage in developing new products.

On the other hand, Vernon's belief that the United States' role in the international economy, to develop and export new products, is not based on any comparative advantage or supply side arguments but on the ease of communication between the potential market and entrepreneur, a demand side argument. In chapter 1, it was pointed out that the theorists who have concentrated on the Heckscher-Ohlin approach, which they modified to bring in human capital, have argued that the United States' relatively abundant factor is human capital, or scientists and engineers. Simply applying the product cycle theory to factor proportions theory indicates that the United States' comparative advantage is in new products. And this approach in itself would resolve the Leontief Paradox. Thus, the product cycle theory does not have to be inconsistent with the new Heckscher-Ohlin approaches. Vernon did not choose this approach; instead he emphasized the differences in the two approaches. Hirsch did attempt to integrate the two approaches, but he needlessly complicated the problem by using three sets of countries, three stages of the cycle, and five factors of production that were not all true factors. Hirsch does not establish a basis for considering "management" or "external economies" as true factors of production. Further, as in most of the previous attempts to apply factor proportions theory, he presents no empirical evidence as to the relative abundance of the various factors of production in the different countries in question. This will be attempted in a later chapter with regard to human capital and unskilled labor.

Actually, with certain modifications the two theories complement each other in a way similar to that in which factor proportions theory complements classical comparative cost theory. Product

8. Hirsch, pp. 33, 38. He presents no evidence that scientists and engineers are the relatively abundant factor of production in the small developed countries other than his own qualitative judgment. However, Hirsch is a scientist from a "small developed country," Israel, who has worked in both the United States and Israel. My findings in chapter 4 also support Hirsch's belief that the smaller developed countries may be able to obtain skilled labor at relatively lower costs than the United States.

cycle theory goes beyond factor proportions theory, broadening
and adding a new dimension, while factor proportions theory goes
beyond classical comparative costs theory by explaining the differing factor productivities that are the basis of trade in the classical
model. The new dimension that is added to the Heckscher-Ohlin
theory is time; a broadening of the theory comes through the explicit recognition of the role of demand. These additions represent
both important and long-needed improvements. However, the product cycle theory as it stands is almost impossible to test empirically,
and is, therefore, "unoperational." This is because subjective as-
sessments are needed to classify the products in their various arbitrary stages. Also, Vernon is guilty of throwing in so many qualitative variables that his theory seems more an ex post description
of a series of events than a general model of international trade.
Therefore, several simplifying assumptions or modifications will be
introduced. These modifications are also an attempt to integrate the
two approaches rather than differentiate them.

The first modification that seems needed is the use of a single
continuous measure instead of the artificial breakdown of the product cycle into three distinct stages, as is done by Vernon and
Hirsch. A diagrammatic representation of the product cycle
adapted from Vernon is presented as Figure 1. The distinguishing
characteristics of the product cycle are the degree of standardization and rate of growth of production. The division of the product
cycle into three stages is quite arbitrary, as Vernon and Hirsch both
admit. A simple measure of the rate of growth of particular industries should be used, rather than their method, to indicate the position on the product cycle curve. This procedure will lend itself
more easily to empirical testing and will be used in chapter 3. An
unstandardized product or rapidly growing industry should be
human capital intensive while a standardized and more slowly
growing industry should be physical capital and unskilled labor intensive.

Given the observation made both by Vernon and Keesing[9] that
physical capital costs about the same internationally and moves increasingly more freely across national borders, the two labor component factors of production probably are more important in determining comparative advantage, as indeed, the classical real cost

9. Vernon, p. 148, and Keesing, "Labor Skills and the Structure of Trade
in Manufactures," in *The Open Economy*, pp. 5–6.

theorists of the nineteenth century thought. Thus, relative factor abundance, especially with regard to skilled and unskilled labor, determines on the supply side which countries are apt to be innovators and which mass producers. Also this theory predicts a systematic change in comparative advantage over time as industries change from skilled labor intensive to unskilled labor intensive.

One point needs emphasis here. Careful use of the definition of factor abundance must be made in testing the factor proportions models. S. Valavanis-Vail first pointed out this problem in conjunction with Leontief's study.[10] The relevant definition is not the quantity or physical definition used by Leontief and others, including the modern skilled labor or human capital approach advocates, Ball and Keesing.[11] A price or economic definition is the correct procedure, although it must be realized, as Jagdish Bhagwati has pointed out, that the price definition "leaves less scope for explanation,"[12] i.e., we get into the explanation at a later step. This definition of relative factor abundance requires the determination of relative wage rates between skilled and unskilled labor. The two definitions will give different results if demand for a physically abundant factor is strong enough to cause that factor to be economically scarce. At this point it is sufficient to point out this refinement and mention that the price definition with regard to human capital has not been used in previous studies on United States comparative advantage. This will be attempted, however, in chapter 4.

Using the price definition of factor abundance introduces the

10. "Leontief's Scarce Factor Paradox," *Journal of Political Economy* 62 (December 1954): 525.

11. Keesing, "Labor Skills and the Structure of Trade in Manufactures," implicitly uses a physical definition of factor abundance, simply assuming that the United States has relative abundances of "supplies of skills [that] afford a factor explanation of trade and location in manufacturing industries within the framework of the Heckscher-Ohlin theory" (p. 5). Ball, "Studies in the Basis of International Trade," pp. 70–72, is more explicit than Keesing. He cites evidence showing that there were more highly skilled workers in the labor force in the United States than in Canada, the United Kingdom, or Argentina. However, Lary, in his study on the comparative advantage of the less developed countries, does present some evidence using the price definition, showing that many countries, including some developing countries, have lower relative prices for skilled labor than the United States. Nevertheless, he does not seem to realize the full implications of these findings (pp. 62–65). This question is analyzed in chapter 4.

12. "The Pure Theory of International Trade: A Survey," *Economic Journal* 74 (March 1964): 20. See also Bo Södersten, *International Economics* (New York: Harper & Row, 1970), p. 68, for an even stronger statement.

demand side into factor proportions theory, but product cycle theory also does this in a more explicit and fundamental way. In the first case, product demand affects factor demand which influences factor cost and comparative advantage. But potential demand through potential profitability also determines what type of products will be innovated and introduced. As per capita income rises, it will become potentially profitable to develop and introduce more products, and the United States is likely to develop these products first since it has by far the highest per capita income. This is Vernon's point, but he does not seem to realize that this implies that few products will be innovated by other countries, since their present per capita incomes were reached and passed perhaps twenty years ago by the United States. Vernon also points out that since labor is the relatively scarce factor of production in the United States, high labor costs should induce labor-saving technological change. Presumably Vernon means unskilled labor here rather than skilled labor. Since economic development is characterized by a substitution of capital, both physical and human, for simple labor, the United States, at the frontier here, also should be leading as innovator of unskilled-labor-saving products and processes. Here again, this leaves little for other countries to innovate since they are lagging behind the United States by ten to twenty years in rising per capita income and increasing labor costs. Therefore, the product cycle theory on the demand side predicts that the United States should innovate the great majority of all new products, since these two categories probably encompass this majority.

As shown by the above model, the product cycle theory does not have to be considered in competition with the conventional approach of international trade theory, despite the initial attempts at differentiation. In fact, the product cycle represents an important and needed contribution to orthodox trade theory that can be easily assimilated into the main body of trade theory. As originally presented, product cycle theory was made needlessly complicated with the result that it was more descriptive than "operationally meaningful." As seen above, though, a simplified product cycle approach can make significant contributions and fit in with modern conventional trade theory and empirical research.

At first view, there also appears to be no statistical conflict between the two approaches, giving further weight to the fruitfulness of synthesizing the two theories. The empirical work cited and presented in chapter 1 generally supports both models. Empirical work has also been accumulated in support of the product cycle model. The results generated can be shown to support the human capital approach of the Heckscher-Ohlin theory as well as the simple model presented above. The empirical work that exists in support of the product cycle will be described briefly, and then a general test of both theories will be presented in chapter 3.

The empirical studies are of two types: intensive studies of individual industries that have followed the product cycle model, and extensive studies of the validity of certain hypotheses that form the framework for the theory. Major studies of individual industries have been done by Hufbauer for the synthetic materials industries, Gordon Douglass for the motion picture industry, and Hirsch for the electronics industry.[13] The authors all conclude that their statistical findings support their own particular variations of the product cycle theory. Hufbauer's version of the product cycle deserves special mention because he completely rejects the Heckscher-Ohlin theory on both theoretical and empirical grounds.[14]

As pointed out in chapter 1, Hufbauer criticizes Minhas' findings of factor intensity reversals between Japan and the United States along the same lines as Ball,[15] and concludes, "we shall accept the assumption that commodities can be unambiguously classified according to factor-intensity" (p. 21). However, he goes on to reject factor proportions theory on a demonstration that the assumptions of similar technologies and constant returns to scale do not hold, for example, between the United States and Japan. But if technologies differ sufficiently, one cannot expect the strong factor intensity assumption to hold unless technologies are neutrally different.[16] For one to support the strong factor intensity theorem and yet maintain that trade is based on different technologies, it must be established that (1) different industries within a country use different levels of technology, (2) different countries use different technologies for

13. See Hufbauer, *Synthetic Materials and the Theory of International Trade*; Douglass, "Product Variation and International Trade in Motion Pictures" (Ph.D. diss., Massachusetts Institute of Technology, 1963); and Hirsch, *Location of Industry*.

14. He states (p. 21), "Considering the weak empirical evidence for the assumptions of equal technology and constant returns to scale, the theory is not promising as an explanation of synthetic materials trade."

15. See chap. 1n26.

16. See p. 10.

the same industry, and (3) with regard to the second point, those technologies must be neutrally different, not biased in the directions of labor or capital saving. The first two assumptions are directly analogous to the assumptions necessary to establish trade based on factor proportions. The third is necessary because if different technologies are differently biased, then factor intensity reversals may be expected to occur. Hufbauer does not mention, let alone establish, grounds for any of these assumptions, although the first two assumptions seem reasonable. Minhas and the Stanford group did find in fitting their CES production function to international data that inter-country differences in the efficiency of factor use were neutral.[17] However, more sophisticated versions of the CES production function have shown definite biases in technology intertemporally and internationally. Yahr shows that when labor skills are introduced into the CES model, countries with a relative abundance of skilled labor tend to substitute labor for physical capital.[18] P. A. David and Th. van de Klundert used a factor-augmenting model of the CES production function which allows one to estimate the elasticity of substitution and the bias of technological progress simultaneously. They identified, for the United States during the period 1899–1960, three distinct stages of widely different biases, ranging from significantly labor-saving during the period 1900–1918, and even more so in 1946–60, to neutral from 1919 to 1945.[19] Finally, in a recent article, C. E. Ferguson and John Moroney identify seven industries of the twenty two-digit SIC industries for the United States as capital using and four as labor using for the period 1948 to 1962, using the techniques developed by David and van de Klundert.[20] Thus, the assumption that technology differs neutrally between countries and over time is questionable.

One is led to expect that if technological differences are great, the differences must be biased in different ways in different industries, and should lead, therefore, to factor intensity reversals. The evidence examined in chapter 1 that supports the strong factor in-

17. Minhas, *An International Comparison of Factor Costs and Factor Use,* p. 51.

18. "Human Capital and Factor Substitution in the CES Production Function," p. 98.

19. "Biased Efficiency Growth and Capital-Labor Substitution in the U.S., 1899–1960," *American Economic Review* 55 (June 1965): 357–94.

20. "The Sources of Change in Labor's Relative Share: A Neoclassical Analysis," *Southern Economic Journal* 35 (April 1969): 308–22.

tensity theorem also supports indirectly the assumption of similar levels of technology. Hufbauer's emphatic support of the strong factor intensity assumption and his model of trade which rejects factor proportions and is based on differing technologies seem to be inconsistent, and are probably wrong in light of the evidence for the strong factor intensity assumption.

Hufbauer's demonstration that leads him to reject the factor proportions theory is a simple comparison between United States and Japanese wage-to-profit ratios. He notes that the differences between the wage-profit ratios in the two countries are far greater than the differences in the capital-labor ratios.[21] Thus, he claims the differences must be due to something other than differing factor proportions. He deduces that the unexplained differences must be due to the use of different technologies, and completely ignores the role of human capital which could easily explain the large differences he observed in the wage-profit ratios and the small difference in the (tangible) capital-labor ratios. Inasmuch as human capital is far more important in the United States than in Japan,[22] the inclusion of human capital would treat a greater part of wages as returns to human capital in the United States than in Japan. This portion, then, should be added to profits. Also, the ratio of total capital to simple labor would be increased to a larger extent in the United States than in Japan because a greater amount of human capital would be added to the United States' figure. Thus, Hufbauer's lack of knowledge of the modified Heckscher-Ohlin approach leads him to reject factor proportions theory. This is understandable, as his Cambridge dissertation was written before the human capital approach became popular.

21. He calculates that the capital-labor ratio in the United States must be at least twice that of Japan, given the existing wages per man-year differences, $5,000 to $1,000, and the existing share of profits in output of 25 per cent and 35 per cent in the two countries. If the United States capital-labor ratio were twice that of Japan's, Japan's share of profits would have to be over 42½ per cent. These calculations are based on the fact that if technologies are equal, the sum of the total of wages and profits must be everywhere equal. Hufbauer, then, rejects the assumption of equal technologies because there is no evidence that capital-output ratios vary that much in the industrial sector (pp. 18–20).

22. The Harbison index of human capital is 261.3 for the United States and 111.4 for Japan. The index is based on pupils currently enrolled in secondary and college-level schools as a percentage of their respective school-age populations. See F. Harbison and C. A. Myers, *Education, Manpower, and Economic Growth: Strategies of Human Resource Development* (New York: McGraw-Hill Book Co., 1964), pp. 31–32.

Starting from this point, Hufbauer develops a technological gap and economies-of-scale trade theory which has many similarities to the product cycle theory. He states that high wage countries will adopt new technologies first. His proof is that high wages reflect high productivities, and high productivities "can ordinarily be traced to longstanding differences in the application of science to industrial problems" (p. 30). This boils down to the extrapolation that countries that have innovated in the past will be the ones that will innovate in the future. This does not offer much new information. As in the product cycle theory, the technological gap theory predicts that slowly the advantages held by the innovating high wage nation will be supplanted by low wage nations that imitate the new technology. Hufbauer found that most of the trade in synthetic materials could be explained by technological gap and scale economy theory, leaving very little for the factor proportions theory to explain (p. 110). His evidence rests on the fact that the advanced nations' exports were "heavily biased in favor of new products by comparison with the exports from other countries" (p. 111). His techniques involve the identification of the major innovations in the synthetic materials field and the determination of the year and country for each innovation. Unfortunately, it would be difficult to apply this method to an industry-wide test of the product cycle theory. There is also the problem of possible biases in determining which innovations to investigate. Hufbauer's theoretical structure is weakened by his failure to explain why high wage countries should be expected to continue to be leading innovators and the fact that the product cycle would not occur according to his model if low wage countries should happen to be the innovators. This is mainly due to his lack of attention to human capital. However, his empirical work does lend strong support to the product cycle model as outlined above, at least for synthetic materials trade.

Hirsch's study of the electronics industry also fits the product cycle model and is consistent with the modified factor proportions approach. He identified six major product groups within the electronics industry (sic 36) and found that (1) the sectors that grew most rapidly also were the ones in which the United States possessed a competitive advantage; (2) the maturity of the sector was negatively correlated with the United States' trade balance in that sector; and (3) the fastest growing sectors which presumably are in their early stages of the life cycle tended to be more labor and skill intensive and less physical capital intensive (pp. 62–82). He concludes, "The findings suggest that the competitive advantage which the U.S. has in electronic products is dynamic in nature. As specific product groups assume more mature characteristics, as the production process becomes more stable, as specifications become more standardized, and importance of the skill content declines, foreign manufacturers are likely to import the production technology, adapt it to their environment, and, in time, provide stiff competition to U.S. manufacturers in their own market" (p. 82). These conclusions are based on only one industry, and, indeed, on only part of that industry.

In addition to industrial studies supporting the product cycle theory, there have appeared recently tests of its hypotheses that cover all of the manufacturing sector. William Gruber, Dileep Mehta, and Raymond Vernon have found a strong link between United States R & D effort and export performance.[23] Dividing nineteen industries into the five most R & D intensive and the fourteen others, they found that the former group of industries accounted for 72.0 per cent of the nation's exports of manufactured goods but only 39.1 per cent of the nation's total sales, and 89.4 per cent of the nation's total R & D expenditures and 74.6 per cent of the company-financed R & D expenditures (p. 24). These findings are, of course, consistent with the product cycle view of the United States as the leading innovator and exporter of new products. They are also consistent with a prediction of the factor proportions theory: because, presumably, the United States' relatively most abundant factor of production is skilled labor and scientists and engineers in the extreme, the United States' comparative advantage is in industries that make the most intensive use of this factor.

Another significant finding of the Gruber study is that the correlations between research effort and export performance weaken as United States trade is limited successively to the more developed

23. "The R & D Factor in International Trade and International Investment of United States Industries," *Journal of Political Economy* 75 (February 1967): 20–37 (hereafter cited as Gruber et al.). The authors calculated Spearman rank coefficients for nineteen industries, ranging from +.69 to +.79, between two measures of research effort, total R & D expenditures as percentage of sales, and scientists and engineers in R & D as a percentage of employment, and two measures of export performance, exports as percentage of sales and excess of exports over imports as percentage of sales. All the coefficients are significant at the 1 per cent level.

countries, until the coefficients lose their significance at the .05 level with West Germany and the United Kingdom (pp. 25–27). The more developed countries would be expected to import the United States' new products first, but also to begin production of them at home first since their demand patterns are the most similar to those of the United States. Gruber et al. present evidence to support the proposition that this is due to United States firms' investments in Europe in the industries in which those firms have export advantages but fear losing them.[24] However, the factor proportions theory also predicts this result since the factor endowments of West Germany and the United Kingdom, including skilled labor, are probably the most similar to those of the United States in comparison with the rest of the free trading world.

In the same issue of the *Journal of Political Economy* in which Gruber et al. appeared, Keesing presented some statistical results quite similar to the findings of that group.[25] Keesing, perhaps the major developer of the skilled labor factor proportions theory of trade, seems in this article to switch sides, joining the ranks of product cycle theorists. He comes to this conclusion because he finds that scientists and engineers in R & D as a percentage of the labor force of each industry "explain" competitive trade success in manufacturing industries considerably better than any other variable tested (p. 46). For eighteen industries in 1961 he calculated a linear correlation coefficient of +.88, and a Spearman coefficient of rank correlation of +.94 between the R & D effort in 1961 and United States exports as a percentage of the group of ten exports for 1962 (p. 39). He checks to see whether physical capital requirements, natural resources, labor skill requirements, or economies of scale are also correlated with his measure of export performance. He finds that physical capital is correlated negatively with export performance, that natural resource intensive industries can be eliminated without affecting the results, that other skill groups exhibit high correlation coefficients with export performance, but not as high as scientists and engineers engaged in R & D, and that value added per establishment (a measure of economies of scale) is also positively correlated with export performance (p. 43). He concludes that his

24. Page 32. This result might also be due to an inadequate breakdown of the commodity categories.
25. "The Impact of Research and Development on United States Trade," pp. 38–48.

findings are "consistent with a view that the world economic role of the United States involves the systematic export of new products" (p. 45). This is not inconsistent with a human capital approach but does indicate that it is not the whole explanation. Also, if one considers that the most human capital intensive factor of production is

TABLE 4.—RESEARCH EFFORT AND WORLD TRADE PERFORMANCE BY UNITED
STATES INDUSTRIES, 1962

INDUSTRY NAME AND SIC NUMBER	RESEARCH EFFORT (Scientists and engineers in R & D as a percentage of total employment)	EXPORT PERFORMANCE (Excess of exports over imports, as percentage of sales)
Food (20)	0.3	−1.2
Tobacco (21)	0.2	2.1
Textile (22)	0.3	−1.1
Apparel (23)	°	−2.1
Lumber and wood (24)	°	−6.2
Furniture and fixtures (25)	0.2	°
Paper (26)	0.3	−3.5
Printing and publishing (27)	0.2	1.1
Chemicals (28)	4.1	4.5
Petroleum and coal (29)	1.8	−0.8
Rubber and plastic (30)	0.5	1.3
Leather (31)	0.1	−3.4
Stone, clay, and glass (32)	°	−0.2
Primary metal (33)	0.5	−1.8
Fabricated metal (34)	0.4	0.7
Machines (non-electrical) (35)	1.4	11.4
Electrical machinery (36)	3.6	2.9
Transportation (37)	3.4	4.1
Instruments (38)	3.4	3.2
All 19 industries:	1.1	0.6
5 industries with highest research effort	3.2	5.2
14 other industries	0.4	−1.1

SOURCE: Gruber et al., "The R & D Factor in International Trade and International Investment of United States Industries," p. 23 (material adapted from Table 1).
°Less than 0.05 per cent.

scientists and engineers engaged in R & D, then one would expect, according to factor proportions theory, that of all the skill groups, scientists and engineers would be the most highly correlated with export performance.

To compare the results generated when a measure of research effort is correlated with competitive trade performance, with the results from the human capital approach used in chapter 1, Table 4 is derived from the Gruber et al. article. It presents their indices of research effort and export performance for all twenty of the SIC industries except SIC 39, miscellaneous manufacturing (they did not calculate R & D effort for this industry). Table 5 shows Spearman coefficients of rank correlations for the nineteen industries calculated by Gruber et al. for 1962, and by the writer, using in addition Tables 1 and 2 for the 1960 and 1965 data. Keesing's study could not be compared with the one in chapter 1, since he did not use the SIC breakdown in the eighteen industries he analyzed.

The results show only a marginally higher association between scientists and engineers in R & D as a percentage of the labor force and 1960 export performance (as measured by exports minus imports), and average annual wages (our proxy for human capital intensity). The Spearman correlation coefficients were +.757 for the first association and +.734 for the second. For the same index of research effort and the 1965 indices of trade performance, net exports and net exports as a percentage of shipments, the Spearman coefficients were +.534, and +.614, and for 1965 average annual wages and the indices of trade performance the associations were +.334, and +.464, somewhat larger spreads. Table 5 also shows that in between those years, in 1962, Gruber et al. calculated a Spearman coefficient of +.691 for the above indices of research effort and export performance as measured by net exports minus imports divided by sales. According to Keesing, the use of 1962 R & D data to explain trade performance in 1960 and 1965 should not affect the correlations since the "structure of R & D expenditure by industry and the pattern of American competitive export performance have been quite stable in recent years" (p. 39). The significant correlations seem to support this belief for these years. The strong influence that natural resources may have on the competitive position of an industry that was discovered for the Heckscher-Ohlin model[26] is also evident in these data, although the effect in the product cycle case is not as strong. The elimination of the four industries, identified as natural resource influenced, that was performed in chapter 1 has also been performed here. Table 5 shows that when SIC 21, 26, 29, and 33 are eliminated, the correlation between human capital intensity and export performance increases from

26. See p. 15.

TABLE 5.—SUMMARY OF COEFFICIENTS OF RANK CORRELATION BETWEEN INDICES OF TRADE COMPETITIVENESS AND MEASURES OF HUMAN CAPITAL INTENSITY AND RESEARCH EFFORT

	INDICES OF TRADE COMPETITIVENESS				
	19 industries			16 industries	15 industries
	1960 net exports	1962 net exports as % of sales	1965 net exports	1965 net exports as % of shipments	1965 net exports as % of shipments minus 3 industries[a]	1965 net exports as % of shipments minus 4 industries[b]
1962 scientists and engineers in R & D as % of the labor force (research effort)	+.757**	+.691**	+.534*	+.614**	+.794**	+.834**
1960 average annual wages (human capital)	+.734**	+.560**				
1965 average annual wages (human capital)			+.334	+.464*	+.865*	+.935*

SOURCE: The coefficient for 1962 net exports as a per cent of sales and 1962 scientists and engineers in R & D as a per cent of the labor force is from Gruber, Mehta, and Vernon, "The R & D Factor in International Trade and International Investment of United States Industries," p. 22n. All the other coefficients were calculated by the author from Tables 1, 2, and 4.
* Significant at the .05 level.
** Significant at the .01 level.
[a] The three industries eliminated were paper (26), petroleum and coal (29), and primary metals (33).
[b] The fourth industry eliminated was tobacco (21).

+.464, to +.935, while the relation between research effort and export performance rises a less startling amount, from +.614 to +.834. The reason for the reversal in the size of the two respective correlation coefficients seems to be that a lower degree of R & D effort is associated with the natural resource influenced industries than would be expected from their human capital intensity. The lack of R & D effort in these industries is a little surprising, since one might expect that cost pressures arising from the exhaustion of domestic natural resources would lead to innovations in those industries similar to those experienced in England before the Industrial Revolution.[27] But in this case, it may have been easier to import the needed materials than to invent new techniques. Since these industries tend to be mature industries, this is further evidence for the product cycle hypotheses. If we are looking for a theory that explains all of the United States' manufactures exports, the product cycle appears to be stronger, at least for 1965, than the factor proportions approach.

However, the fact remains that for 1960 the results only slightly favored the research effort measure, while for 1965, the larger difference is reversed when natural resource influenced industries are eliminated. Thus, neither theory yet appears significantly stronger on empirical grounds.

There has appeared one other study purporting to test some of the other product cycle hypotheses. Louis Wells' main finding was that the United States' export performance, as measured by the ratio of 1962–63 average exports by value to 1952–53 average exports, was highly correlated with the income elasticity of ownership for twenty consumer products for which he could gather the necessary data.[28] His measure of income elasticity of ownership is calcu-

27. See Paul Mantoux, *The Industrial Revolution in the Eighteenth Century* (New York: Harper & Row Publishers, 1961), pp. 189–338, for an excellent account of the cost pressures that built up in the various industries that led England into the Industrial Revolution and the inventions that were successively introduced to meet these pressures. Other reasons for the lack of R & D effort in these industries may be the oligopolistic nature of many of these industries and the Adams and Dirlam argument cited in chapter 1 (n36) or the government induced concentration of R & D in the national defense industries at the expense of the others, discussed in chapter 5.

28. "Test of a Product Cycle Model of International Trade: U.S. Exports of Consumer Durables," *Quarterly Journal of Economics* 83 (February 1969): 152–62. The correlation coefficient was +.896. Wells in his summary of the product cycle theory did not mention Vernon's hypothesis that the United States should also have an export advantage in labor-saving capital goods.

lated from United States data, but he shows that rankings of the degree of saturation of various consumer products by households are quite similar between the United States, the United Kingdom, the European Economic Community, and Israel (p. 156). These results, according to Wells, support Vernon's hypothesis that the United States has a strong propensity to innovate and produce products that satisfy wants connected with high incomes. However, he seems to be concluding too much from his data, because one would expect that for the rest of the world, the marginal propensity to import (which is what Wells' export performance index really is measuring, given rising world per capita income) would be highly correlated with United States income elasticity. Wells' procedure is more of a test of the similarity of international demand structures than of the product cycle theory.

In addition, the use of factor proportions theory might also explain these results if products with a high income elasticity also tend to be human capital intensive. Unfortunately, Wells does not provide a list of the products that he tested, but a priori this hypothesis seems likely. Products that appeal to high income receivers are apt to be more sophisticated and more highly engineered than products that are income inelastic and, thus, would require higher human capital inputs in both production and marketing. Note the difference between a high quality piece of stereo equipment and a lower priced phonograph. More fundamental than this, though, is the fact, pointed out above, that almost all new products will be highly income elastic with a high initial price and high human capital intensity. Therefore, Wells' finding is also consistent with a theory that predicts that a country with a relative abundance of human capital, especially scientists and engineers, will be a leading innovator and exporter of relatively new products.

Wells finds support for the product cycle model in one other phenomenon. He notes that for a given product, the relative difference between expensive and inexpensive variations of that product are usually less in the United States than in Germany and Japan, and he attributes this to the product cycle prediction that "The United States would have comparatively lower costs due to savings from the economies of scale resulting from production of luxury versions for a larger home market" (p. 158). But once again the Heckscher-Ohlin model predicts the same result. Luxury versions should be human capital intensive relative to cheaper versions of the same product, and the United States presumably has a comparative advantage in human capital intensive goods.

This brief summary of the empirical studies that support the product cycle thesis shows that most of the results generated also support the human capital approach of the Heckscher-Ohlin theory. Thus, a synthesis of the two approaches is seen to be consistent with the empirical work that supports both theories. The product cycle approach adds the dimension of time to conventional factor proportions theory and strengthens the mechanism whereby demand patterns influence trade patterns. There is also some evidence that the role of the United States as an exporter of new products is reinforced by its high per capita income and large market size as well as its favorable factor proportions.

At the same time, both theories have been set up by different authors to stand by themselves. But when the factor proportions theory stands alone, it becomes static and emphasizes mainly the supply side. When the product cycle theory stands alone, it must depend more on differing technologies, economies of scale, and marketing problems. There is some evidence that these last three factors do play a role, especially in specific instances, but not enough yet to reject the general validity of the factor proportions model if it too is consistent with the same empirical observations that support the product cycle theory. Without the factor proportions theory, the product cycle model is still dynamic and gives equal weight to the demand and supply sides. Its major shortcomings are that it is less esthetically pleasing, more complicated, and harder to test empirically than the factor proportions theory.

However, chapter 3 will present empirical evidence as to the comparative "explanatory" power of the major hypotheses of each theory. The same industries will be used to test both theories and the major tests will cover the whole manufacturing sector of the United States rather than selected industries or products as has been done in the past, especially by product cycle supporters. Although the case has been built that the two theories are perfectly consistent with each other, this hypothesis has been mostly conjecture. Thus, a more detailed, empirical study, aimed specifically at testing this hypothesis and the synthesis of the human capital factor proportions and product cycle models, seems needed.

3. Results of Statistical Tests

THE TWO major theories purporting to explain the United States' international trade patterns in manufactures will now be examined empirically, the examination to cover the entire range of United States manufactures at the two-digit level of classification developed by the Department of Commerce.

A major criticism of most investigators of the empirical basis for the product cycle theory is that they examined only particular industries in a case study method or chose only particular groups of industries. A major criticism of the investigators of both theories is that they concentrated on particular years. In this investigation four years and all twenty two-digit industries will be examined. Further, this marks the first time that one set of data has been used to examine both theories. It is hoped that this study will allow us to reach some conclusions about the relative merits of the two theories, and about whether they are competing or complementary, as set forth in chapter 2.

The procedure employed is to identify certain variables as characteristic of the product cycle theory or the factor proportions theory. Some of these variables have been identified and used in previous studies and some are new. These variables will be compared with two measures of export performance, exports minus imports (X_1), and exports minus imports as a percentage of total shipments of that industry (X_2). These two variables have been calculated for the years 1958, 1960, 1965, and 1966 by the writer and are presented in Table 34 in the appendix. The calculations are based on the Department of Commerce unadjusted total export and import data along commodity lines, in contrast to Ball's use of Department of Labor data for 1960 which "adjust" imports to eliminate those imports of products that do not compete with United States production. The data used in this study have not been "adjusted," as it is felt that all imports of manufactured goods represent at least potential, if not actual, competition to United States manufactured products. Any attempt to define which products are actual competitors and which are not must necessarily be artificial and subjective.[1]

TESTS OF THE HECKSCHER-OHLIN MODEL

Variables that have been used in previous studies testing the human capital Heckscher-Ohlin approach are labor skills by Keesing, Waehrer, and Ball, and wages and salary value added per employee by Lary. The results of the former group's studies have been reported in chapter 1. Lary only proposed and calculated his measure—he did not test it. This was done briefly in chapter 1, and the results indicate that the variables examined are positively related to export performance, with labor skills (L–S) having a stronger relationship than either the human or physical capital intensity variables as measured by Lary's method of wages and salary value added per employee (W & S) and non-wage value added per employee (N–W & S). Although Lary's measures are not as strong proxies for human capital as the labor skills approach, his method does have the advantage, as he points out, of being more readily available. His measures can be calculated from census data for all recent years and down to the four-digit level. The labor skills data are available only for 1960 and 1950, and for all two- and a few selected three-digit level industries. The value added method also has the advantage of describing the intensity of three different factors of production, physical capital, human capital, and labor.

Several other proxies for human capital were examined but also suffered the handicap that the data needed to calculate them are available only every ten years. The additional variables that were calculated over the two-digit industries from 1960 data are the median school years completed by the male labor force (M) and the percentage of the labor force that has completed five or more years of college (C). The male labor force median (M) was used because a total labor force median is not available. The five years of college completed index was used on the assumption that the statistic that measures the greatest degree of human capital intensity should be the best proxy for overall human capital built up by formal education. A measure that attempts to add together differ-

1. For discussion and criticism of this procedure see p. 15.

ent degrees of human capital intensity would be the ideal one, but this would involve too many problems that have not been completely solved yet. For example, would college years of education be counted as twice as important or valuable as grade school years, or vice versa? One weighting scheme is to allow the market to decide, and this is implicit in the wages and salary per worker index that has already been described and used. The problems associated with this index, relating to imperfections in the labor market, have been discussed. Second, a simple average could be used which implicitly assumes that different years of schooling are equivalent. Variable M is such an average, although an imperfect one.

Finally, one problem with index C is that it counts only formal education as human capital, leaving out on-the-job training, which Jacob Mincer has calculated represents "a very large component of total investment in education in the United States economy. Measured in terms of costs, it is as important as formal education for the male labor force."[2] Thus, index C is an imperfect measure of human capital to the extent that the distribution of on-the-job training differs from the distribution of formal education. However, Mincer has found that on-the-job training and formal schooling are significantly complementary. For 158 occupations he found a rank correlation coefficient of +.86 between estimates of school and on-the-job training requirements.[3] Therefore, there is reason to expect that index C should be a fairly good proxy for human capital. However, the labor skills variable (L–S) may pick up some human capital, especially of the self-made manager type, through the simple occupational classifications approach, which the formal education variable would not include.

These five indices were calculated for the twenty two-digit industries and appear as Table 35 in the appendix. Tables 6 and 7 summarize the results of calculating rank and simple linear correlation coefficients between the above variables and the two measures of export performance for the year 1960. The results from the

2. "On-the-job Training: Costs, Returns and Some Implications," *Journal of Political Economy* 70 Supplement (October 1962): 73.
3. Ibid., p. 60. One would also expect that other types of human capital such as health expenditures and moving expenses would be correlated with investment in education, since investment in education would increase the return to the other types of human capital. For a discussion of the complementarity between investments in health and education, see Selma J. Mushkin, "Health as an Investment," ibid., pp. 130–32.

rank correlation table indicate that the labor skills variable is slightly more strongly related to export performance than median years of education or the percentage of the labor force with at least five years of college. All three human capital variables are significant at the .01 level. Below this tier, the wage and salary variable was significant at the .05 level on both counts, while the proxy for physical capital was not significant. Thus, if the United States' comparative advantage does lie in human capital intensive goods, pre-

TABLE 6.—SPEARMAN CORRELATION COEFFICIENTS BETWEEN FACTOR INTENSITY VARIABLES AND INDICES OF EXPORT PERFORMANCE FOR 1960

	X_1	X_2
N–W & S	.123	.311
W & S	.426*	.467*
L–S	.635**	.675**
M	.611**	.612**
C	.617**	.641**

*Indicates significance at the .05 level.
**Indicates significance at the .01 level.

TABLE 7.—SIMPLE LINEAR CORRELATION COEFFICIENTS BETWEEN FACTOR INTENSITY VARIABLES AND INDICES OF EXPORT PERFORMANCE FOR 1960

	X_1	X_2
N–W & S	.090	.190
W & S	.466*	.471*
L–S	.528**	.589**
C	.403*	.470*

*Indicates significance at the .05 level.
**Indicates significance at the .01 level.

sumably imperfections in the labor market prevent the flow of wages and salary per employee from being as good an indication of the stock of human capital as the labor skills and education indices.

The results from the linear correlation coefficient table modify these conclusions somewhat. The labor skills index remains significant at the .01 level, but the education index C falls to the .05 level of significance along with the wages and salary per employee variable. Again, the index of non-wages and salary per employee was not significant. The labor skills approach does definitely seem to be the better "predictor" of United States comparative advantage, but again, its usefulness is hampered by its lack of availability for non-census years and more detailed industrial classifications. However, a Spearman coefficient of +.950 between the 1950 and 1960 percentages of professional, technical, and kindred workers to total employment indicates that the 1960 skill index can be taken as a good proxy for immediately surrounding years. A skill index was estimated for 1965 by extrapolating the trend from 1950 to 1960 on to 1965. The method of extrapolation is given by the formula

$$L\text{--}S_{65} = \frac{1}{2}\left[\frac{L\text{--}S_{60}}{L\text{--}S_{50}} - 1\right] + L\text{--}S_{60}$$

where the subscripts stand for years. The labor skills indices for 1950, 1960, and 1965 are presented in Table 36 in the appendix.

Several other years were then examined. The Bureau of the Census' annual publication *U.S. Commodity Exports and Imports as Related to Output* began in 1960 with 1958 data, and the September 1968 issue contains 1966 data, so these years as well as 1965 were chosen and examined more closely. Table 37 in the appendix shows the 1958, 1965, and 1966 W & S and N–W & S indices that were calculated by the writer from the various years of the *Survey of Current Manufactures*. An additional variable, value added per employee (VA), a measure of the total of human and physical capital, was also calculated and is presented in Table 37. Table 8 presents the Spearman coefficients between the two measures of export performance and the indices for the three additional years examined.

Table 8 bears out the strong performance of the labor skills variables. The $L\text{--}S_{65}$ variable does perform slightly better than the $L\text{--}S_{60}$. This table, in conjunction with Table 6 showing the 1960 Spearman coefficients, reveals that there has been a steady rise in the correlation coefficient between non-wage and salary value added per employee, and export performance, so that by 1965 and 1966, physical capital seems to be rivaling human capital as measured by W & S as an explanation for export performance. In fact the value added per employee index, a proxy for total capital, becomes significant at the .05 level in 1965 and 1966 when correlated with exports minus imports divided by shipments. Value added per employee also outperforms the W & S variable for these two years, especially for 1966.

Table 9 completes the examination of the "explanatory" power of the variables associated with the Heckscher-Ohlin theory in predicting export performance by examining the linear correlation coefficients between factor intensity variables and 1965 export performance. The variables W & S, $L–S_{60}$, and C retain about the same "explanatory" power despite the use of 1960 data in calculating

TABLE 8.—Spearman Correlation Coefficients Between Factor Intensity Variables and Indices of Export Performance for 1958, 1965, and 1966

	1958		1965		1966	
	X_1	X_2	X_1	X_2	X_1	X_2
N–W & S	.089	.280	.245	.483	.089	.417*
W & S	.430*	.468*	.347	.487*	.308	.418*
VA/L	.114	.280	.292	.523*	.171	.484*
L–S[a]	.603**	.654**	.550**	.719**	.553**	.665**

*Indicates significance at the .05 level.
**Indicates significance at the .01 level.
[a]$L–S_{60}$ was used for 1958, while $L–S_{65}$ was used for 1965 and 1966.

TABLE 9.—Simple Linear Correlation Coefficients Between Indices of Factor Intensity and Indices of Export Performance for 1965

		1965	
		X_1	X_2
1965	N–W & S	.129	.263
1965	W & S	.410*	.479*
1965	VA/L		.335
1960	L–S		.577**
1965	L–C	.482*	.608**
1960	C		.445*

*Indicates significance at the .05 level.
**Indicates significance at the .01 level.

$L–S_{60}$ and C. However, the correlation coefficients between $L–S_{60}$ and C and 1965 export performance fall slightly compared to 1960, while for W & S it rises. However, the use of the $L–S_{65}$ index does result in a slight improvement over $L–S_{60}$. Both N–W & S and VA/L show improvements as they did in the rank correlation coefficient analysis, but not by as much as in the non-parametric case, indicating that a linear model may not describe the relationship between the physical capital to labor ratio and export performance as well as another model. One reason for the poor results of N–W & S in the linear model may be the very large amount of physical capi-

TABLE 10.—REGRESSION RESULTS OF VARIOUS HECKSCHER-OHLIN MODELS USING 1965 DATA AND X_2 AS THE DEPENDENT VARIABLE

#	a	L–S	W&S	N–W&S	D	R	S̄	F
(1)	−2.582	.3159 (.1681) .05	.001458 (.06010) >.25	.000830 (.001119) >.25		.608	3.23	3.13 >.05
(2)	−2.609	.3168 (.1626) .05	.002645 (.05622) >.25			.608	3.14	4.99 .05
(3)	−2.405	.3228 (.09933) .005				.608	3.05	10.56 .01
(4)	−9.408	.005029 (.1768) >.25	.09816 (.06360) .10	.008027 (.009995) .25	−5.375 (2.070) .01	.752	2.78	4.88 .05
(5)	−10.740		.1260 (.03220) .005		−5.432 (1.602) .005	.735	2.68	9.99 .01
(6)	−1.736	.3585 (.0935) .005			−2.995 (1.607) .05	.689	2.87	7.67 .01

NOTE: The numbers in parentheses below the partial regression coefficients are standard errors. The numbers below the standard errors and the F statistic are levels of significance.

tal per employee associated with the petroleum industries (SIC 29), which also had a relatively high negative trade balance. In 1965, the physical capital per employee ratio was 2.52 standard deviations above the mean for the petroleum industry, and 2.06 standard deviations above the mean for tobacco, the second most physical capital intensive industry. The industry with the lowest physical capital intensity, apparel, was only 1.00 standard deviations below the mean. Thus, an important finding from this study, aside from the general support it provides for the human capital approach to trade theory, is the recent tendency for physical capital intensity to become more highly associated with industries in which the United States has a comparative advantage. This may mean that a Leontief-type test performed today may not show the same results as before. Evidence examined later on will support this thesis.

Finally, several multiple regression models were examined to see if more than one factor of production was determining United States export performance. The two factors of production chosen to be examined were human capital to simple labor intensity and physical capital to simple labor intensity. The labor skills index and the wages and salary index both serve as proxies for human capital. Due to imperfections in the labor market, wages and salary are an imperfect index of human capital intensity, but one which is available for more industries, years, and countries than the labor skills index. The second factor of production is represented by non-wages and salary value added per employee. The regression equations and results are presented in Table 10.

Regression models (1) and (3) indicate that one factor, labor skills, explains most of the variance in export performance as measured by 1965 exports minus imports divided by shipments (X_2).[4] In the three equations, only the partial regression coefficient to L–S is significant. About 36 per cent of the variation in X_2 can be "explained" by the human capital index (L–S), and the physical capital index adds little or nothing to the explanatory power of the factor intensity model. The W & S index also loses its significance when combined with L–S.

However, these conclusions are modified somewhat when a dummy variable (D) signifying natural resource intensity is added.

4. Results similar to those that follow were also obtained when exports minus imports (X_1) was regressed on the factor intensity variables and when X_1 and X_2 were regressed on the factor intensity variables using 1960 data.

The procedure followed was to assign these to SIC 20, food and kindred products, SIC 26, paper and allied products, SIC 29, petroleum and coal products, and SIC 33, primary metal products, and zeroes to the remaining sixteen industries. The basis of classification is completely subjective, and different writers might come up with different assignments; this fact must be kept in mind when analyzing the results. The addition of the dummy variable in equations (4) through (5) does significantly improve the fit of the regression model. The adjusted standard error of estimate is reduced from 3.05 in model (3) to 2.68 in model (5). Also, the dummy variable is significant at low levels in all three cases. Equation (4) indicates that the coefficient to L–S loses significance when combined with W & S, N–W & S, and D, while W & S and N–W & S attain significance for the first time at .10 and .25, respectively. Although the best statistical fit is obtained by model (5), model (6), which uses L–S and D as independent variables, is superior in a theoretical sense since L–S is thought to be a better measure of human capital intensity than W & S.

Human capital intensity does seem to be a good indicator of export performance. The Heckscher-Ohlin model is also measurably improved when account is taken of natural resource influenced industries. Also, note that the physical capital index does have the expected sign, and does become significant at the .25 level when the natural resource influence is added. Finally, the matrices of the simple correlation coefficients for 1960 and 1965 are presented in the appendix in Tables 38 and 39. Note that in all cases except for the dummy variable, L–S is more highly correlated with the other independent variables than with either dependent variable for both years. There seem to be only two factors of production, human capital and natural resources, which are clearly associated with United States export performance.

The results of the preceding tests of the human capital modified Heckscher-Ohlin model seem to indicate that the human capital approach does have definite validity in explaining United States export performance in manufactures, especially when the influences of natural resources are taken into account. A similar procedure was also used in testing the product cycle model. Certain variables that have been identified as product cycle variables and several new ones will be examined in conjunction with the two indices of United States trade performance.

TESTS OF THE PRODUCT CYCLE MODEL

Both Gruber et al. and Keesing, as reported in chapter 3, have used scientists and engineers engaged in research and development (S & E) as a variable to indicate the United States' propensity to develop new products.[5] The product cycle model holds that the United States' comparative advantage lies in new products.[6] The variable, S & E, as calculated by Gruber et al. for 1962, is also used in this study but with one slight modification. Since Gruber et al. did not provide an estimate for SIC 39, miscellaneous manufacturing, a value of .3 was assigned to SIC 39 so that the results obtained with this variable would be comparable with the other variables which cover twenty industries. The value .3 is the percentage of workers engaged in research, development, and testing to total employment, as calculated by the writer from 1963 census data. The main difference in the two definitions is that some employees engaged in research, development, and testing may not be scientists and engineers, but the difference should not be enough to distort the results.

The next variable selected was one that indicates the recent rates of growth of the various two-digit industries. The index chosen was 1965 value added divided by 1947 value added times one hundred (VA).[7] The product cycle model predicts, as illustrated in Figure 1, that the most rapidly growing industries are likely to be industries that are in the new product stage, the stage at which the United States can be expected to hold a comparative advantage.[8] As industries mature and products become standardized and stable, growth rates and export performance are expected to decline.

The product cycle theory further predicts that the United States should develop new products and processes that are either income elastic or labor saving or both, since the United States has the highest per capita income and the highest labor costs in the world. Products with high income elasticities should also have the highest growth rates during the rapid growth of the postwar period and,

5. See chap. 2nn23, 25.

6. See p. 19.

7. Other periods of time for VA were used with results similar to those that are reported in this chapter.

8. This is based on the assumption that industries have similar growth rates over their product cycle, so that at a given point in time, an industry growing rapidly relative to other industries is also growing rapidly relative to its own product life cycle.

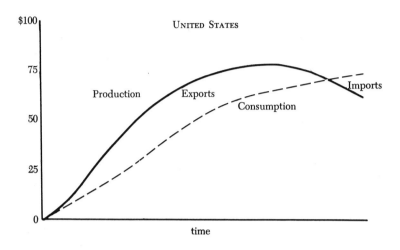

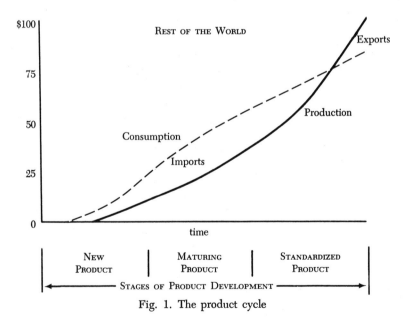

Fig. 1. The product cycle

therefore, the VA variable should be a good surrogate for income elasticity. It is not a perfect substitute, of course, since relative supply conditions have changed among industries in the postwar period. But to the extent that long-run industry supply curves are elastic (i.e., constant costs), the VA index will be a good proxy for income elasticity. The study by Wells of selected products lends some support to the notion that the United States should have a comparative advantage in products with high income elasticities.[9] Since there are no known estimates of income elasticity at the two-digit level, our VA index will have to suffice. The product cycle model as proposed by Vernon also maintains that the United States' labor costs are the highest in the world. Therefore, according to the product cycle model, industries in which technological progress has been biased toward labor-saving techniques or industries, where the rate of growth of labor efficiency has exceeded the rate of growth of capital efficiency, should also be industries in which the United States enjoys a comparative advantage. In these industries, technological progress is likely to have originated in the United States, while in industries where improvements in capital efficiency exceed those in labor efficiency, the technological progress is more likely to have originated in Europe or Japan where physical capital costs are more important relative to labor costs. The industries in which the United States is the leader in the development of new technology should also be industries in which United States export performance is high according to the product cycle theory.

An index of the rate of growth of labor efficiency minus the rate of growth of physical capital efficiency for the twenty two-digit industries in the United States over the period 1948–62 has recently been provided by Ferguson and Moroney.[10] These estimates, henceforth called L–C, were calculated from regression coefficients derived by using the David–van de Klundert formulation of the factor-augmenting CES production function.[11] This procedure fits by classical least squares the logs of the capital-labor ratio to the logs of the wage-profit ratio and to time, t, for each of the twenty industries over the sixteen-year time span. The results of Moroney and

9. However, see pp. 35–36 for a criticism of his methods.
10. "The Source of Change in Labor's Relative Share."
11. For a further discussion on the procedure see ibid., pp. 313–16, and David and van de Klundert, "Biased Efficiency Growth and Capital Labor Substitution in the United States."

Ferguson's regressions are presented along with S & E and VA in Table 40 in the appendix.

Rapidly growing firms and industries are also apt to have several other characteristics, according to the product cycle model. Those whose growth is based on new products and techniques should have a high profits-to-sales ratio due to their temporary monopoly positions in new products and production techniques.[12] New and rapidly growing industries should also have higher than average depreciation rates due to the widespread use of accelerated depreciation accounting methods. Finally, these industries and firms may be expected to rely heavily on the services of outside firms in advertising, publicity, legal advice, research and development, and general advisory and professional matters. Both Vernon and Hirsch have pointed out that the availability to United States firms of these external economies (i.e., specialized and technical services) gives the United States a strong comparative advantage in the development of new products and techniques.[13] Finally, royalty payments and patent fees, travel and communications expenses, and entertainment and miscellaneous other expenses should be high for new firms that face little price competition and are intent on maximizing growth rates.

The Census Bureau of the United States Department of Commerce publishes an index every five years that measures these factors. The index is the cost of materials and payroll to total value of shipments. This index for 1963 (O/S) is presented in Table 40. Since cost of materials plus value added equals shipments, and value added can be divided into payroll plus non-payroll value added expenses, then 1 minus the O/S index will be a measure of the product cycle characteristics listed in the preceding paragraph, plus a few other factors such as property taxes and rents. Lary has broken down into its component parts non-payroll value added in all United States manufacturing enterprises for 1957. Non-payroll value added was $55.9 billion in 1957, of which the product cycle categories mentioned made up $47.8 billion, or about 86 per cent of the total. The remaining $8.1 billion included property taxes, insurance, rent, and maintenance and repair services purchased from other firms, items which should not vary systematically with the rate of growth of firms or the introduction of new products (p.

12. See pp. 19–20.
13. See p. 22.

34). Therefore, the O/S variable is taken as a composite index which reflects various hard-to-measure characteristics of the product cycle. The index should be inversely related to export performance.[14]

The product cycle model also has a place for economies of scale. The model predicts that in those industries where there are significant economies of scale, the United States' comparative advantage will be maintained for a longer period of time through the product life cycle. To test this hypothesis two indices of economies of scale were calculated: the first (ES_1) is simply 1963 value added per establishment computed from the 1963 *Survey of Current Manufactures*, and the second is the 1958 ratio of value added per employee for firms with over 250 employees to value added per employee for firms with only one to nine employees (ES_2). These indices also appear in Table 40. However, the economies-of-scale hypothesis of the product cycle model was quickly rejected, since the Spearman rank and simple linear correlation coefficients between ES_1 and the 1965 export performance index, X_2, were found to be +.134, and +.124, respectively, while the Spearman coefficient between ES_2 and 1965 X_2 was only +.065. The signs are in the direction expected but the correlation coefficients are not close to being significant.

However, the other product cycle variables generated better results. Tables 11 and 12 present the Spearman and linear correlation coefficients between the first four product cycle variables, S & E, VA, L–C, and O/S, and the export performance variables, X_1 and X_2, for various years. In comparing Tables 11 and 12, an interesting reversal is immediately apparent. The VA variable is significantly correlated with the two export performance measures for all four years at the .01 level under the rank correlation method, and is also appreciably higher than the Spearman correlation coefficient between S & E and the eight export performance indicators. However, these findings are partially reversed when linear correlation

14. Since one of the measures of export performance chosen is exports minus imports divided by shipments (X_2), and since the O/S variable may be expressed as shipments minus non-wage value added divided by shipments, possible problems of "spurious" correlation must be examined. For a brief discussion of the problem of "spurious" correlation, see Taro Yamane, *Statistics, An Introductory Analysis*, 2d ed. (New York: Harper and Row, Publishers, 1967), pp. 460–61. The problem arises since the variable "shipments" appears both in the dependent and in the independent variable. However, since "shipments" appears in both the numerator and the denominator of O/S, any possible bias is mitigated. But more important is the fact that X_2 is negative almost half of the time and, therefore, any bias should cancel out.

coefficients are compared. In three of the four cases, the linear correlation coefficients between S & E and the X's are greater than between VA and the X's; in one case, that of the 1965 X_2, the VA measure is slightly greater. This last observation is important since the X_2 measure, which adjusts for industry size, is a better indicator of export performance than X_1, while 1965 is the later of the two years. The fact that Spearman and linear coefficients differ to such

TABLE 11.—SPEARMAN COEFFICIENTS BETWEEN PRODUCT CYCLE VARIABLES AND INDICES OF EXPORT PERFORMANCE

	1958		1960		1965		1966	
	X_1	X_2	X_1	X_2	X_1	X_2	X_1	X_2
S&E	.552**	.605**	.537**	.613**	.492*	.602**	.433**	.531*
VA	.657**	.695**	.632**	.705**	.559**	.656**	.556**	.635**
L–C	.194	.298	.215	.283	.298	.356	.286	.369
O/S				−.588**		−.553**		−.613**

*Indicates significance at the .05 level.
**Indicates significance at the .01 level.

TABLE 12.—LINEAR CORRELATION COEFFICIENTS BETWEEN PRODUCT CYCLE VARIABLES AND INDICES OF EXPORT PERFORMANCE

	1960		1965	
	X_1	X_2	X_1	X_2
S&E	.627**	.619**	.533**	.573**
VA	.473**	.543**	.396	.577**
L–C	.181	.186	.250	.298
O/S			−.380	−.554**

*Indicates significance at the .05 level.
**Indicates significance at the .01 level.

a degree indicates that some model other than a linear model might be indicated.

The evidence from the Spearman tests and the linear evidence for 1965 seem to indicate that the rate of growth of an industry is a slightly better indicator of a strong export performance than the percentage of scientists and engineers engaged in research and development.

The next product cycle variable tested, the rate of growth of labor efficiency minus the rate of growth of physical capital efficiency (L–C), was not significant in any of the twelve cases at the .05 level. However, the signs were all in the direction expected, and the coefficients were steadily increasing in size through time so that the Spearman coefficient between 1966 X_2 and L–C was only .008 away from significance at the .05 level. Thus, there seems to be a slight bit of evidence to indicate that industries that are characterized by labor-saving technological growth also tend to be industries in which the United States has a strong export performance.

The broad-based O/S variable, cost of materials plus payroll divided by shipments, was found to be significant at the .01 level with X_2 in both the linear and Spearman cases. Evidently, profits, depreciation, and purchases from other firms of technical and professional services are related to export performance as is predicted by the product cycle model.

As with the factor intensity variables, measures of export performance were regressed on various product cycle models. Table 13 presents the results of regressing 1965 exports minus imports divided by shipments, X_2, on various combinations of the four product cycle variables.[15]

When the full four-variable product cycle model, equation (7), was used, about 55 per cent of the variance of X_2 was explained. However, the partial regression coefficient to VA was not significant even at the .25 level. Also this model did not generate the lowest adjusted standard error of estimate, $\overline{S}$, and, therefore, did not have the highest adjusted $\overline{R}^2$. Equation (8) which regresses X_2 on S & E, L–C, and O/S produced the best fit. About two-thirds of the observations fell within 2.78 percentage points of the regression line and the three partial regression coefficients had the expected signs and were significant at levels ranging from .025 to .10. After models (7) and (8), model (10), which uses only two independent variables, S & E and O/S, presented the next best fit with an $\overline{S}$ of 2.90 and both partial regression coefficients being significant at the .05 level.

It is apparent from the regression equations that there is a high degree of multicollinearity between VA and S & E. Table 41 in the appendix presents the matrix of the simple linear correlation coefficients. Only between S & E and VA is the correlation coefficient between the independent variables higher than between the dependent variable, X_2, and the independent variables. Therefore, it seems that VA and S & E are measuring much of the same factor.

---

15. The export performance variable X_1 was also regressed on various product cycle variables using 1965 data, and X_1 and X_2 were regressed on the product cycle variables using 1960 data. The results are similar to those that are reported below.

TABLE 13.—Regression Results of the Product Cycle Model Using 1965 X_2 as the Dependent Variable

#	a	S&E	VA	L-C	O/S	R	S̄	F
(7)	12.79	.8845 (.5766) .15	.005694 (.008941) >.25	23.59 (15.22) .10	−19.76 (12.36) .10	.740	2.83	4.54 .05
(8)	16.23	1.169 (.4979) .025		23.84 (14.93) .10	−22.45 (11.40) .05	.732	2.78	6.15 .01
(9)	−3.704	.9388 (.7082) .15	.01058 (.008809) .15	25.75 (15.90) .10		.686	2.97	4.75 .05
(10)	17.59	1.125 (.5193) .025			−24.31 (11.85) .05	.680	2.90	7.29 .01
(11)	−5.238		.01903 (.006213) .005	24.61 (16.22) .10		.643	3.03	5.98 .05
(12)	−1.192	1.554 (.4951) .005		26.88 (16.08) .10		.650	3.01	6.24 .01

NOTE: The numbers in parentheses below the partial regression coefficients are standard errors. The numbers below the standard errors and the F statistic are the levels of significance.

This is to be expected since there should be feedback in both directions between rapid growth and a high research and development effort.

The VA variable is also important for another reason, even if it is highly correlated with S & E. The S & E variable is only available at a high level of aggregation and only for a few years. However, the VA variable can be calculated down to the four-digit level and is available for all postwar years in the United States and a great many other countries. Using VA as a product cycle proxy can be likened to Lary's use of wages and salary per worker as an approximate, but readily available, index of human capital intensity. However, the VA variable does seem to have explanatory power in its own right. This proposition will be further supported later in the chapter.

Note that in all the product cycle models the partial regression coefficient of L–C is significant at the .10 level and that L–C is one of the three independent variables in model (8) which was the product cycle model attaining the best fit (smallest standard error) with X_2. Thus, a labor-saving bias does seem to be associated with United States export performance. A lack of correlation between L–C and VA and S & E (.028 and −.017 respectively) is perhaps surprising. The rationale for expecting that an index of growth of labor efficiency minus capital efficiency be associated with export performance is that the United States is more apt to develop labor-saving techniques (in comparison with the rest of the world) than capital-saving technology since labor costs are so much higher in the United States. Thus, one would expect that scientists and engineers engaged in R & D would be heavily concentrated in these industries. However, since development and applied research accounted for 96 per cent of total expenditures on R & D in 1962 and pure research only 4 per cent,[16] and since probably as much development effort is required in adopting foreign technology as in adopting home produced technology, the lack of association between S & E and L–C can be explained. Also working against the expected correlation is the fact that much of R & D effort is centered around developing new consumer goods rather than more efficient production techniques.

Therefore, at least three factors seem to be influencing United

16. National Science Foundation, *Basic Research, Applied Research and Development in Industry, 1962* (Washington, 1965), p. x.

States export performance in the product cycle model. The United States' propensity to develop new, presumably income elastic, consumer products and labor-saving capital goods and techniques in conjunction with an abundance of external economies provides the United States with an initial comparative advantage in both new consumer and capital goods.

Tests of the Combined Heckscher-Ohlin Product Cycle Model

Thus, it appears that the product cycle model also "explains" United States comparative advantage fairly well. It will be recalled that the thesis has been developed that the product cycle model and the human capital Heckscher-Ohlin model do not have to be considered inconsistent or competing theories and that, indeed, the product cycle model could be considered as a broadening or expansion of the Heckscher-Ohlin model because it adds the dimension of time and the demand side to the conventional model. It was also pointed out that most of the product cycle advocates have denied this link between the two models. The link that was proposed that could be used to combine the two models so that equal weight is given to the supply and demand sides rests on two propositions. The first is that new products tend to be human capital intensive, and the second that human capital is the United States' relatively most abundant factor of production.[17] Therefore, a high correlation between human capital intensity and the product cycle variables, especially in the "new product" variables (S & E and VA), would be expected. Our best index of human capital intensity was found to be the percentage of the labor force engaged in professional, technical, and kindred occupations (L–S). Wages and salary per worker (W & S) has also been used as a proxy for human capital intensity. Indeed, Table 38 indicates that the correlations between per cent of labor force with at least five years of college (C) and L–S and W & S were .937, and .745, respectively, using 1960 data.

Table 42 in the appendix presents the matrix of simple linear correlation coefficients for both the factor intensity and product cycle variables. The table indicates that all four intercorrelation coefficients between the two human capital variables and the rapid growth and new-product product cycle variables are significant at the .01 level and greater than the corresponding four correlation

17. The validity of the first proposition is examined in this chapter; the second is assumed for now but examined in detail in chapter 4.

coefficients with the dependent variable X_2. The best index of human capital intensity, L–S, has a correlation coefficient of .735 with VA, and .870 with S & E. Thus, there does appear to be a definite link between the two models. Human capital intensity and the propensity to develop new products are more highly associated with each other than either is with export performance. This leads one to propose that perhaps there are not twin factors operating on the demand and supply side affecting United States export performance, but that one factor, either supply or demand, is affecting the other two. Perhaps the abundance of human capital gives the United States a comparative advantage in human capital intensive products, and since new products tend to be human capital intensive, there is an appearance that the propensity to develop new products is a causal factor in determining United States trade structure. This argument can also be turned around with the United States' propensity to develop new products due to a high per capita income being the causal factor for both an abundance of human capital and in the structure of United States trade. Since L–S is slightly more highly correlated with X_2 than with VA or S & E, there is slightly more evidence for the former explanation.

However, the broader explanation of both a demand and supply side interaction is more appealing on purely theoretical grounds. Therefore, we proceed to test the synthesized model using multiple regression techniques in the rest of the chapter. Indeed, when multiple regression analysis is used to combine variables from the two models, slightly better results are obtained than when the two models are tested in isolation. Also, further modification in the tests, which will be performed later, causes the results of the synthesized model to be significantly better than the results for the separate models. Table 14 lists the results of performing least squares regressions for various mixed models, and, for convenience, reproduces the product cycle and factor intensity models that generated the best fits with X_2 (1965). The models are listed in order of the smallest adjusted standard errors of estimate which is taken as the single best criterion for the closeness of the regression relationship.

The model that best explains export performance is a mixed model (13) that contains one factor intensity and two product cycle variables, L–S, O/S, and L–C. All three partial regression coefficients are significant at at least the .05 level, and the adjusted

TABLE 14.—COMPARISON OF THE HECKSCHER-OHLIN, PRODUCT CYCLE, AND MIXED REGRESSION MODELS

Type	#	a	L-S	W&S	N-W&S	D	VA	S&E	O/S	L-C	R	S̄	F
M	13	13.70	.2714 (.0927) .005						−20.47 (10.70) .05	27.93 (14.10) .05	.770	2.60	7.78 .01
M	14	10.73	.2795 (.0934) .005						−16.29 (11.64) .10	25.78 (14.34) .05	.785	2.61	6.02 .01
H–O	15	−10.74		.1260 (.0322) .005		−5.432 (1.602) .005					.735	2.68	9.99 .01
M	16	9.43	.2558 (.1317) .05			−1.531 (1.670) .20	.002305 (.008741) .25		−15.21 (12.68) .10	25.33 (14.90) .10	.786	2.70	4.53 .05
H–O	17	− 9.41	.00503 (.1768) .25	.09816 (.0636) .10	.00803 (.00999) .25	−5.375 (2.070) .01					.752	2.78	4.88 .05
P–C	18	16.23						1.169 (.498) .025	−22.45 (11.40) .05	23.84 (14.93) .10	.732	2.78	6.15 .01
P–C	19	12.79					.00569 (.00894) .25	.8845 (.6766) .15	−19.76 (12.36) .10	23.59 (15.22) .10	.740	2.83	4.54 .05

TABLE 14—*Continued*

Type	#	a	L-S	W&S	N-W&S	D	VA	S&E	O/S	L-C	R	S̄	F
H-O	20	-1.74	.3585 (.0935) .005			-2.955 (1.607) .05					.689	2.87	7.67 .01
P-C	21	17.59						1.125 (.5193) .025	-24.31 (11.85) .05		.680	2.90	7.29 .01
P-C	22	-3.70					.0106 (.00881) .15	.9388 (.7082) .15		25.75 (15.90) .10	.686	2.97	4.75 .05
H-O	23	-2.41	.3228 (.0993) .005								.608	3.05	10.56 .01
M	24	.71	.2121 (.1463) .10				.00948 (.00920) .20				.638	3.05	5.83 .05
P-C	25	25.43							-32.11 (11.80) .01		.613	3.13	5.11 .05
H-O	26	-2.61	.3168 (.1626) .05	.00265 (.0562) .25							.608	3.14	4.99 .05

NOTE: The numbers in parentheses below the partial regression coefficients are standard errors. The numbers below the standard errors and the F statistic are levels of significance.

standard error of estimate ($\overline{S}$) is 2.60. The next best fit is also produced by a mixed model (14) which is similar to the first but contains the natural resource dummy as a fourth independent variable. However, the third best model is the Heckscher-Ohlin model with two independent variables, W & S and D. The adjusted standard error of estimate rises to 2.68 in this model and both variables are significant at the .005 level. However, as pointed out above, on theoretical grounds, this is not the best Heckscher-Ohlin model since labor skills have been shown to be a better proxy for human capital than average wages and salary. The Heckscher-Ohlin model with L–S and D as independent variables (20) has an $\overline{S}$ of 2.87, which places it behind several product cycle models. Leaving out the possibly subjective dummy variable, labor skills alone produce an $\overline{S}$ of 3.05.

In examining the increased explanatory power of the mixed model over the separate models, there are several ways to proceed. First, simply by observing the results of the various models, we can conclude that the combined or mixed model does explain more of the variance but not much more than either the best H-O or product cycle models. The problem, of course, is the multicollinearity, especially between S & E and labor skills. However, the improvement that substituting L–S for S & E brings—compare (13) with (18)—is encouraging and seems to indicate that an abundance of human capital does contribute to the United States' net export performance in manufactures.

A more objective way to proceed is to use analysis of variance (ANOVA) to determine if the mixed model does significantly add to our knowledge of the variance of the dependent variable. Our models cannot be compared directly since in most cases the various sums of squares are not independent, and are, therefore, not separable and additive. However, in the specific cases where product cycle variables are added to factor intensity variables, or vice versa, the ANOVA test can be used. The problem here is that this does not always compare the "best" Heckscher-Ohlin or product cycle model with the "best" mixed model.

In the case of examining the improvement that the product cycle model brings to the Heckscher-Ohlin model, this problem is not much of a hindrance because the best Heckscher-Ohlin model on theoretical grounds, although not on empirical, is augmented by two product cycle variables. First we use ANOVA to measure the

TABLE 15.—ANOVA TEST OF MODEL (14)

SOURCE OF VARIATION	DEGREES OF FREEDOM	SUM OF SQUARES	MEAN SQUARE
Total	20	280.49	
Explained by Heckscher-Ohlin Model (20), L–S and D	3	140.08	
Additional variation explained by product cycle variables O/S and L–C	2	31.00	15.5
Unexplained variation	15	109.08	7.27

$$F = \frac{15.50}{7.27} = 2.1$$

$$F_{2,\ 15,\ .05} = 3.7$$

contribution of O/S and L–C (14) to the Heckscher-Ohlin model (20) which contains L–S and D as independent variables. Table 15 shows that the additional variance explained by the two product cycle variables is not significant at the .05 level. Table 16 shows the results of adding the same two product cycle variables to labor skills. The additional variables do explain a significant portion of the previously unexplained variance (at the .05 level), and, therefore, we can conclude that the combined product cycle and Heckscher-Ohlin model (13) does significantly improve our understanding of United States export performance over the simple single

TABLE 16.—ANOVA TEST OF MODEL (13)

SOURCE OF VARIATION	DEGREES OF FREEDOM	SUM OF SQUARES	MEAN SQUARE
Total	20	280.49	
Explained by Heckscher-Ohlin model (3), L–S	2	112.5	
Additional variation explained by product cycle variables O/S and L–C	2	59.7	29.8
Unexplained variation	16	108.3	6.8

$$F = \frac{29.8}{6.8} = 4.4$$

$$F_{2,\ 16,\ .05} = 3.6$$

variable factor proportions model (23). The importance of natural resources to the Heckscher-Ohlin model has again been demonstrated.

An ANOVA test to determine whether the combined model significantly improves on the product cycle model was not performed due to the high intercorrelation between S & E and labor skills. Any acceptable product cycle model had to contain S & E as an independent variable, and, therefore, adding labor skills added little explanatory power to the model. A simple comparison between models (18) and (13) does indicate a significant improvement. In this example, L–S replaces S & E in a model in combination with O/S and L–C. This is definite evidence that a model that takes into account both the supply and demand side does improve our understanding of the structure of United States foreign trade.

These conclusions are reinforced by a final modification of the test procedure. It was observed that there was one industry that none of the three model types could explain satisfactorily. The actual value of 1965 X_2 for SIC 35 (machinery except electrical) is 10.32 per cent, while the value estimated by the best regression equation (13) is 2.22 per cent. The calculated value is over three standard errors of estimate above the actual value. Furthermore, this one industry accounted for over 59 per cent of the unexplained variance in model (13).

One possible explanation for the extraordinary export performance of this industry is in line with the product cycle model. The product cycle model predicts that the United States will export labor-saving capital goods, and, indeed, SIC 35 is the one two-digit classification which is made up almost solely of capital goods industries. This single industry accounted for about 23 per cent of the 1965 United States exports of manufactures.[18] An intensive investigation of SIC 35 might be profitable, but it is beyond the scope of this investigation.

Therefore, due to the extraordinary influences operating on this industry, which biased the results of the various models in a downward direction, we proceeded by dropping SIC 35 from our sample and running the regression models again using the nineteen-industry sample. The results are listed in Table 17. The models are again listed in order of lowest standard error of estimate. The improvement in the fits is immediately evident. The adjusted $\bar{R}^2$ for the

18. Calculated from Table 34 in the appendix.

best twenty-observation model (13) was .516, while this same model in the nineteen-observation case (30) produces an adjusted $\bar{R}^2$ of .724.

Table 17 also reveals that the mixed models consistently explain the variations better than the two separate models and that the product cycle models consistently outperform the factor proportions models, reversing the findings for the twenty-observation case. The five best regression models are mixed, as is the seventh best, while the sixth, eighth, and ninth are product cycle models, and the last three are all factor proportions models. The mixed model which explained the greatest amount of variance (27) had an adjusted $\bar{R}^2$ of .718, the best product cycle model (32) had an adjusted $\bar{R}^2$ of .679, and the best Heckscher-Ohlin model (36) had an adjusted $\bar{R}^2$ of .569. The difference between the mixed and product cycle models is not as great as the difference between the product cycle and the factor proportions models. In the nineteen-industry cases the factor proportions model with the best fit now is also the Heckscher-Ohlin model, which was considered the best on theoretical grounds (i.e., L–S + D + N–W & S). Most of the coefficients in the various models are significant at acceptable levels, a marked improvement over the twenty-observation case. The increased significance of the VA variable, especially in comparison with S & E, is also noteworthy.[19]

In the nineteen-observation case, the ANOVA test fits our procedure quite well since the best mixed model (27) contains as subsets the second best Heckscher-Ohlin model (37) and the third best product cycle model (35), models which are not far below the best models in their respective categories in performance. Therefore, two ANOVA tests were performed, one adding the factor proportions variables to the product cycle variables (Table 18) and the second adding the product cycle variables to the factor proportions variables (Table 19). The probability that the additional variation explained by the two Heckscher-Ohlin variables is due to chance is a little greater than 5 per cent. Therefore, we must conclude that the additional 8 per cent of variation explained by the factor proportions model is not significant at the .05 level. However,

---

19. This is significant since the availability of VA is much higher than that of S & E. The use of VA will make it quite easy to identify industries in which the United States should have a comparative advantage according to the product cycle model.

TABLE 17.—COMPARISON OF THE HECKSCHER-OHLIN, PRODUCT CYCLE, AND MIXED REGRESSION MODELS, SIC 35 DELETED

Type	#	a	L–S	W&S	N–W&S	D	VA	S&E	O/S	L–C	R	S̄	F
M	27	5.54	.1735 (.0765) .025			-1.059 (.955) .15	.00654 (.00504) .15		-15.75 (7.22) .025	15.71 (8.67) .05	.901	1.54	11.26 .01
M	28	7.40	.1681 (.0770) .025				.00647 (.00508) .15		-18.74 (6.75) .01	17.04 (8.65) .05	.891	1.55	13.55 .01
M	29	8.84	.2421 (.0567) .0005			-1.043 (.978) .20			-18.68 (7.02) .01	17.29 (8.79) .05	.888	1.57	13.02 .01
M	30	10.63	.2359 (.0567) .0005						-21.59 (6.50) .005	18.58 (8.74) .025	.878	1.58	16.83 .01
M	31	7.95	.2307 (.0630) .005		.00311 (.00648) .25	-1.329 (1.170) .15			-17.45 (7.67) .025	15.97 (9.45) .10	.890	1.62	9.89 .01
P–C	32	8.13					.00847 (.00521) .10	.6458 (.3949) .10	-18.78 (7.17) .01	14.10 (8.99) .10	.877	1.64	11.65 .01
M	33	6.27	.1949 (.1605) .15	-.00102 (.00468) .25		-.8408 (1.446) .25	.00709 (.00611) .15	.00300 (.6302) .25	-15.84 (7.85) .05	15.49 (9.52) .10	.902	1.67	6.84 .01

TABLE 17—Continued

Type	#	a	L-S	W&S	N-W&S	D	VA	S&E	O/S	L-C	R	S̄	F
P-C	34	13.12						1.073 (.310) .005	-22.75 (7.09) .005	14.71 (9.46) .10	.852	1.73	13.21 .01
P-C	35	7.76					.01414 (.00410) .005		-19.35 (7.54) .025	12.97 (9.45) .10	.851	1.73	13.17 .01
H-O	36	-2.78	.2380 (.0699) .005		.0110 (.0069) .10	-3.091 (1.154) .01					.816	1.91	10.00 .01
H-O	37	-2.08	.2886 (.0653) .0005			-2.412 (1.125) .025					.781	2.00	12.49 .01
H-O	38	-3.86	.2329 (.1334) .05	.0246 (.0511) .25		-2.919 (1.560) .05					.785	2.05	8.01 .01

NOTE: The numbers in parentheses below the partial regression coefficients are standard errors. The numbers below the standard errors and the F statistic are levels of significance.

TABLE 18.—Anova Test of Model (27) Which Contains Product Cycle Model (35) and Heckscher-Ohlin Model (37) as Subsets

SOURCE OF VARIATION	DEGREES OF FREEDOM	SUM OF SQUARES	MEAN SQUARE
Total	19	172.63	
Explained by product cycle model (35), VA L–C, and O/S	4	127.63	
Additional variation explained by Heckscher-Ohlin model (37), L–S, and D	2	14.32	7.16
Unexplained variation	13	30.68	2.36

$$F = \frac{7.16}{2.36} = 3.04$$

$$F_{2, \ 13, \ .05} = 3.80$$

when the three product cycle variables are added to the two factor proportions variables (Table 19), the additional 18.5 per cent of explained variation is significant at the .05 level. Therefore, on strict statistical grounds, the product cycle model with the variables VA, L–C, and O/S does add significantly to the knowledge of export performance already gained from the use of a factor proportions model based on human capital and natural resource intensities.

Finally, Table 43 in the appendix presents the matrix of simple correlation coefficients for the nineteen-industry case. The main

TABLE 19.—Anova Test of Model (27)

SOURCE OF VARIATION	DEGREES OF FREEDOM	SUM OF SQUARES	MEAN SQUARE
Total	19	172.63	
Explained by Heckscher-Ohlin model (37)	3	109.78	
Additional variation explained by product cycle model (35)	3	32.17	10.72
Unexplained variation	13	30.68	2.36

$$F = \frac{10.72}{2.36} = 4.6$$

$$F_{3, \ 13, \ 105} = 3.41$$

difference between this table and the one for the full twenty-industry case is that the correlation coefficients between five of the independent variables and the dependent variables increase significantly while the intercorrelation coefficients remain about the same. The variables, L–S, N–W & S, VA, S & E, and O/S, all benefit significantly by the exclusion of industry 35 from the sample. Also note that the product cycle variable VA, an index of the rate of growth of value added, now alone explains 53 per cent of the variation in export performance.

The conclusion that can be drawn is that a synthesized product cycle and factor proportions model does significantly improve our understanding of United States export performance over separate factor proportions and product cycle models. This is true in a formal statistical sense for the mixed models' improvement over various Heckscher-Ohlin models for both the twenty- and nineteen-industry cases. However, this is not true in a formal statistical sense for the mixed models' improvement over the product cycle model although the improvement was close to being significant in the nineteen-industry case. However, there definitely was an improvement, albeit not "significant," when the factor proportions model was added to the product cycle model. Also, the partial regression coefficient of labor skills was significant at the .025 level in the best mixed model for the nineteen-industry case.

The synthesized model which combines the major demand side and supply side theories (the factor proportions and product cycle theories, respectively) thus appears to be an improvement over either single side theory. If one side can be said to have predominant influence, the evidence indicates that the demand side or the product cycle theory has slightly better explanatory power than the factor proportions theory. This is especially evident when the extremely high export surplus of SIC 35 is recalled and the product cycle explanation for this phenomenon is admitted. In fact, it will be argued in chapter 4 that the observed factor proportions might better be viewed as a result of demand patterns rather than as a cause of comparative advantage. The strict supply side factor proportions theory using quantity definitions of factor abundance requires similar demand conditions among countries. This proposition will be examined in chapter 5. Human capital, which is the United States' relatively most abundant factor of production on a quantity basis, may not necessarily be its most abundant factor of production on a price basis. If this is true, we must look beyond the factor proportions theory, either to factors not reflected in prices or wage rates or to the demand side (i.e., the product cycle theory). The factor proportions observed in United States export surplus industries may then be viewed as a result of the human capital intensiveness of new products rather than as an additional influence giving rise to comparative advantage.

4. Evidence on the International Abundance of Human Capital

THE FUNDAMENTAL assumption of the new Heckscher-Ohlin explanation of the trade patterns of United States manufactures is that human capital or labor skills is the United States' relatively abundant factor of production while unskilled labor is the relatively scarce factor of production. This proposition must have seemed so obvious to the early proponents of this approach that they did not even feel the need to make this assumption explicit.[1] Perhaps this is due to the traditional concern of Heckscher-Ohlin theorists with the quantity rather than the price definition of factor abundance. On a quantity definition of factor abundance, the United States certainly does have a relative abundance of human capital. However, for the Heckscher-Ohlin theorem to be valid, the United States must also have a relative abundance of human capital on a price basis. The usual assumption of factor endowment theorists is that there are no demand reversals.

Although the importance of the price definition was first pointed out by Valavanis-Vail and Romney Robinson,[2] the demand side has always been minimized by factor endowment advocates. Perhaps the reasoning for this is that, when stated in terms of factor prices, "the [Heckscher-Ohlin] theorem . . . is not very interesting, because factor prices are themselves results of a complicated interplay of economic forces."[3]

1. For example, see Keesing, "Labor Skills and the Structure of Trade in Manufactures," and Waehrer, "Wage Rates, Labor Skills and the United States Foreign Trade," both in *The Open Economy*, and Kenen, "Nature, Capital, and Trade." However, Ball, "Studies in the Basis of International Trade," p. 26n39, does offer empirical evidence that the United States had an abundance of skilled labor on the quantity definition.

2. Valavanis-Vail, "Leontief's Scarce-Factor Paradox," p. 525, and Robinson, "Factor Proportions and Comparative Advantage: Part I," *Quarterly Journal of Economics* 70 (May 1956): 184–87.

3. Södersten, *International Economics*, p. 68.

Ball seems to have been one of the few trade theorists to have recognized the need to mention something (although only indirectly) about the relative abundance of human capital on the price basis. In the context of trying to explain the "apparent paradox" of the international flow of human capital to the United States despite the fact that the United States' abundant factor of production is also human capital, Ball states: "Because the U.S. is abundantly supplied with both tangible capital and skilled labor, and doubtless for other reasons as well, the U.S. wage of any skill level is higher than the wage of the same skill level abroad, even though the U.S. wage of highly skilled labor may be a lower multiple of the U.S. wage of less skilled labor than the same foreign ratio (the U.S. relative price of skilled labor is lower than the foreign relative price of skilled labor, even though the U.S. absolute price of skilled labor is higher than the foreign)."[4]

There are several interesting aspects to this chain of reasoning that do not fit into the world of a Heckscher-Ohlin theorist. First, the United States' abundance of skilled labor should cause the absolute wage rates of United States skilled labor to be lower than the wage rates of foreign skilled labor, given the assumptions of the factor proportions model. Second, there is still a possible explanation for the opposite finding with regard to wage rates if a third factor, tangible capital, is relatively abundant in the United States and is complementary with human capital rather than a substitute factor. However, the human capital Heckscher-Ohlin theorists have pointed to the similar interest rates among countries and high capital mobility as justification for their down-playing the importance of physical capital as a determinant of trade patterns. And, as pointed out in the earlier chapters, the empirical evidence strongly supports their contention. The importance of human capital has recently been emphasized in a study by Anne Krueger. Using factor proportions assumptions, she finds as a lower bound that "the concept of human capital can explain more than half the difference in income levels between the United States and a group of the less-developed countries for which data are available."[5]

Thus, it must be the "doubtless other reasons" outside the factor proportions theory that explain this unpredicted wage level differ-

4. "Studies in the Basis of International Trade," p. 73.
5. "Factor Endowments and Per Capita Income Differences among Countries," *Economic Journal* 78 (September 1968): 642.

ential. Also note that Ball does not seem to realize that his whole case rests on the fact that the United States' skill differential must be relatively less than the foreign skill differential. This is indicated by his statement quoted previously, "even though the U.S. wage of highly skilled labor *may* be a lower multiple of the U.S. wage of less skilled than the same foreign ratio" (my italics). But again, one should not be too critical of Ball since he did go further on this point than any of the other writers in the Keesing school.

Lary, in developing data to examine the strong factor intensity assumption of the Heckscher-Ohlin theory, also presented some evidence on the spread of wages in different countries, thus crudely measuring the relative price of skilled labor. However, like Ball, he did not seem to realize the full implications of his findings. He states, "It is also interesting to observe, however, that the spread of average wages from Group I to Groups II and III is wider in the United States and Canada, and wider still in Japan than it is in a number of other countries, including some of the less developed countries in addition to Argentina. . . . This subdued variability in wages may bear unfavorably on the ability of such less developed countries to compete in labor-intensive manufactures."[6] Indeed, if Lary's data is correct on Heckscher-Ohlin reasoning, the "subdued variability in wages" would certainly prevent "such less developed countries" from competing successfully in labor intensive products. Lary, being a major advocate of the factor proportions approach, does not seem quite ready to believe his own findings. Certainly he does not give this point the emphasis it deserves. Also, since he is writing mainly from the viewpoint of the less developed countries, he does not seem to realize the implications of his findings for United States comparative advantage.

This chapter will attempt a deeper probe into the empirical basis for the implicit assumption of most Heckscher-Ohlin theorists that the United States' relatively abundant factor of production on the price basis is human capital. First, however, an examination

6. *Imports of Manufactures from Less Developed Countries*, p. 62. Lary's observation is made from a series of twenty graphs which are not accurate enough to allow numerical analysis. The three groups are Lary's breakdown of the twenty industries in the International Standard of Industrial Classification into three categories according to their United States wage level (pp. 62–66). This, in fact, biases the spread of wage rates in the other countries toward a narrower range since their low wage industries may not be the United States' low wage industries. This bias, although not mentioned by Lary, may explain his failure to draw out the full implications of his findings.

of factor abundance on the quantity definition will be presented. The new Heckscher-Ohlin theorists have not empirically established this even more basic assumption beyond a few general observations. The probable reason for this most likely is the lack of comparable census data on an international scale. However, this deficiency has recently been rectified by the publication by the Organization for Economic Cooperation and Development of a volume of statistics on the occupational and educational structure of the labor force in fifty-three countries.[7] This volume attempts to make the occupational structure by sector of the labor force comparable using the International Standard Classification of Occupations system (ISCO). For our purposes, the percentage of skilled labor to semiskilled and unskilled in manufacturing (International Standard of Industrial Classification #2–3) was thought to be the best measure of a country's endowment of skilled labor, and, therefore, the percentage of ISCO #0 (professional, technical, and related workers) in manufacturing to the total workers in manufacturing was calculated for the forty-four countries for which comparable data were available.[8] The results appear in Table 20.

The results support the assumption by the advocates of labor skills that the United States has a relatively large endowment of highly skilled labor, although not as strongly as was implied by their apparent feeling that empirical evidence was not necessary. Leaving out the Communist countries, only Sweden's labor force in manufacturing is more heavily weighted with skilled labor than that of the United States, although France, Finland, the United Kingdom, Canada, and Germany are not far behind.

Another measure of skill endowments, ISCO #0 as a percentage of total workers, was calculated for all sectors of the economies of each of the forty-four countries, and the results also appear in Table 20.[9] It was thought that the total factor endowment of a country,

7. *Statistics of the Occupational and Educational Structure of the Labour Force in 53 Countries* (Paris: OECD, 1969).

8. An occupational approach to human capital estimation was chosen over a measure of educational level since the OECD study did not attempt to make the educational attainment levels of the different countries comparable. Also the labor skills approach has been traditionally used by writers in this field, and in chapter 3, I experimented with several educational attainment measures which did not predict the United States' comparative advantage as well as the occupational approach.

9. The other sectors in addition to manufactures in the ISIC system are agriculture, mining, construction, electricity, commerce, transportation, and service.

TABLE 20.—Physical Skilled Labor Endowments of 44 Countries

Country	Skill Endowment Iᵃ (per cent)	Skill Endowment IIᵇ (per cent)
Sweden	9.57	11.54
Rumania	7.60	6.05
United States	7.45	11.09
France	7.26	9.93
Hungary	7.15	7.20
Finland	6.49	8.20
United Kingdom	5.44	8.52
Canada	5.26	9.72
Germany	5.14	7.68
Netherlands	4.35	9.13
U.S.S.R.	4.23	8.77
Norway	3.95	8.05
Israel	3.20	12.08
Panama	3.09	5.87
Argentina	3.05	6.03
Belgium	3.02	8.32
Mexico	3.02	3.62
Denmark	2.63	7.52
Greece	2.33	4.25
Puerto Rico	2.14	7.86
South Africa	2.10	2.81
Taiwan	1.93	3.49
Japan	1.78	4.89
Ireland	1.67	6.69
Uruguay	1.61	6.08
Pakistan	1.40	5.51
Chile	1.36	4.95
Egypt	1.24	3.20
Uganda	1.22	7.23
Turkey	1.21	1.71
Costa Rica	1.21	5.22
Peru	1.19	3.66
Hong Kong	1.08	4.74
Philippines	.94	2.94
South Korea	.93	2.36
Zambia	.90	7.14
El Salvador	.85	2.89
Portugal	.79	2.78
Honduras	.42	2.52
Jamaica	.41	3.05
Sierra Leone	.27	1.22
Syria	.21	2.33
Ecuador	.17	3.26
Ghana	.16	2.34

Source: Calculated by the writer from OECD, *Statistics of the Occupational and Educational Structure of the Labour Force in 53 Countries,* Table IA, pp. 16–276.
ᵃProfessional, technical, and related workers in manufacturing as a percentage of total workers in manufacturing.
ᵇProfessional, technical, and related workers in all sectors as a percentage of total workers in all sectors.

TABLE 21.—PERCENTAGE OF BREAKDOWN OF LABOR REQUIREMENTS BY SKILL CLASS[a] TO PRODUCE 1962 EXPORTS OF 14 COUNTRIES, USING 1960 UNITED STATES SKILL COMBINATIONS FOR 46 MANUFACTURING INDUSTRIES

	I	II	III	IV	V	VI	VII	VIII	INDEX[b]
United States	5.02	2.89	2.74	4.85	8.38	14.96	15.73	45.73	.654
Sweden	3.53	2.34	2.23	4.41	8.92	18.87	13.73	45.96	.547
Germany	3.89	2.48	2.33	4.69	8.44	15.84	14.54	47.79	.541
United Kingdom	3.77	2.99	2.36	4.79	7.20	15.01	14.41	49.68	.484
Switzerland	3.50	2.39	2.18	5.29	7.76	12.66	15.65	50.56	.473
Canada	4.17	2.33	2.43	4.76	5.39	16.45	14.70	49.76	.467
Netherlands	3.62	2.39	2.31	4.65	5.04	15.62	14.50	51.87	.418
France	3.15	1.92	2.15	4.58	5.28	15.55	14.14	53.24	.370
Austria	2.76	1.76	1.91	4.15	5.71	15.97	12.87	54.87	.338
Belgium	2.83	1.71	1.98	3.86	4.67	17.35	12.75	54.85	.323
Italy	2.75	1.75	1.97	4.33	4.32	12.78	13.24	50.86	.293
Japan	2.48	1.66	1.78	3.96	4.56	15.15	12.04	58.38	.281
India	0.71	0.58	1.06	3.47	1.33	11.13	9.62	72.09	.084
Hong Kong	0.69	0.49	1.13	3.75	1.34	8.48	10.39	73.73	.084

SOURCE: Keesing, "Labor Skills and the Structure of Trade in Manufactures," in *The Open Economy*, Table 2, p. 14.
[a]Skill classes are: I, scientists and engineers; II, technicians and draftsmen; III, other professionals; IV, managers; V, machinists, electricians, and tool- and diemakers; VI, other skilled manual workers; VII, clerical, sales, and service workers; VIII, semiskilled and unskilled workers.

[b]Index is computed from the formula Index $= \dfrac{2(I+II+III)+V}{VIII}$

not just the composition of the labor force in manufacturing, should be the basis of comparative advantage according to the Heckscher-Ohlin theory. The United States is again third with 11.09 per cent of its labor force falling in the category of professional, technical, and related workers, but on this measure, Israel surpasses Sweden as the country with the most skill abundant labor force and Rumania drops behind the United States. Again this indicates on factor proportions grounds that the United States' comparative advantage lies in skill intensive products.

The development of these data allows us to test the labor skills approach in a way that has not been attempted yet. This test extends the human capital approach to countries other than the United States. Keesing has developed for a set of countries estimates of skill requirements necessary for producing their exports on the assumption that their skill requirements are the same as those of the United States.[10] Table 21 presents the skill index that Keesing calculated from their skill requirements for the fourteen countries for which he calculated his index. There are ten countries in Keesing's sample that overlap with the forty-four countries found in Table 20. Spearman rank correlation coefficients were then calculated for the Keesing skill index and the two physical endowments indices. The coefficient for the test of association between the estimated skill requirements and the actual physical skill endowments in manufactures was +.830, which is significant at the .01 level, while the Spearman coefficient for the skill requirement index and physical skill endowments for the whole economy was +.697, which is significant at the .05 level.

This test indicates that Keesing's assumption that United States skill requirements are a good proxy for foreign skill requirements seems to be valid and that countries with increasingly abundant endowments of skilled labor export increasingly skill intensive manufactured products. Both propositions strongly support the Heckscher-Ohlin-Keesing theory. It is not unexpected that the relationship between the Keesing skill index estimated from trade patterns and the skill index estimated from the skill intensity in the manufacturing sector is stronger than the relationship between the Keesing skill index and the factor endowments index for the whole economy. In a skill abundant country the manufacturing sector

10. See "Labor Skills and the Structure of Trade in Manufactures," pp. 8–13, for a discussion of this procedure.

which competes internationally should be more skill intensive than the sectors of the economy which do not compete internationally, i.e., construction, electricity, commerce, transportation, and services. Bhagwati also makes the point that "factor-abundance comparisons should refer to the quantities of factors employed in the traded-goods sector, since the original formulation of the Heckscher-Ohlin theorem is logically deduced in a framework assuming no non-traded goods."[11] Thus, further support on an international scale seems to have been generated for the Heckscher-Ohlin theory.

However, we will now examine the assumption basic to the Heckscher-Ohlin theory, that the association between factor abundance and factor intensity of exports must rest on the lower relative costs of the abundant factor. We wish to determine if a country exports products which are intensive in its abundant factor of production on a price or relative cost definition. Therefore, we need an international compendium of comparable skill differentials, i.e., the ratio of skilled to unskilled workers' earnings, or the variations among countries in inter-occupational earnings structures. The greater the skill differential or the greater the variation in earnings, the cheaper unskilled labor is relative to skilled. Thus, countries with high skill differentials or large variation in their earnings structures should have a comparative advantage in the production of unskilled labor intensive goods. There are a few scattered international skill differential statistics but little data on earnings by occupations translated into the isco system. However, the International Labor Office does publish data on earnings by isic industry. Furthermore, the literature on income distribution and on the "brain drain" has been tapped to provide information on the relative factor abundance of skilled labor on the price definition.

The Inter-Industry Variation of Earnings

One method of estimating the inter-occupational variation of earnings is to use the inter-industrial variation of earnings as a proxy under the assumption that the skill mix of corresponding industries does not differ appreciably among different countries. The inter-industry wage structure, given competitive markets, would be equal to the inter-occupational wage structure times the skill mix of industries. This is true because the average wage of a given industry

11. "The Pure Theory of International Trade," p. 22.

is equal to the sum of the average wage of each occupation times the percentage of workers in that occupation employed in the given industry. In equation form this is

$$(1) \qquad W_i \; = \; \sum_{j=1}^{n} \frac{w_{ij}q_{ij}}{N_i}$$

where W_i is the average wage of industry i, w_{ij} is the average wage of occupation j in industry i, q_{ij} is the number of workers in occupation j employed in industry i, and N_i is the total number of workers in industry i. The assumption of competitive labor markets gives us $w_{1j} = w_{2j} = w_{3j} = \ldots w_{mj}$ for i=1 to m. In other words, workers of the same skill get the same wages in whatever industry they are employed. The assumption of competition in domestic markets is, of course, basic to the Heckscher-Ohlin model, as is the assumption, which is also needed, that production functions are identical in all countries. The Keesing advance of the Heckscher-Ohlin theory makes the additional assumption that "the same industries are skill-intensive relative to other industries in all countries."[12] This is the assumption of no factor intensity reversals. In terms of equation (1), the assumption means that a ranking of United States industries on the ratio $\frac{q_{11}}{N_i}$, where occupation 1

is (say) the most skilled, should be highly correlated with other countries' rankings on this same factor.[13] For support of the assumption of no factor intensity reversals, Keesing cites the strong evidence of consistencies in wage rates in international comparisons.[14] In addition, one of the most thorough studies yet completed in this area concludes that "there is a remarkable similarity in the order of ranking of industries according to their earnings in developed countries."[15]

12. "Labor Skills and the Structure of Trade in Manufactures," p. 8.

13. Since more than one set of rankings is possible because j is likely to be greater than 2, a coefficient of concordance would be a better statistic than a coefficient of rank correlation.

14. Some of this evidence is in Yahr, "Human Capital and Factor Substitution in the CES Production Function," and Waehrer, "Wage Rates, Labor Skills, and the United States Foreign Trade," both in *The Open Economy*; and Minhas, *An International Comparison of Factor Costs and Use*.

15. T. S. Papola and V. P. Bharadwaj, "Dynamics of Industrial Wage Structure: An Inter-Country Analysis," *Economic Journal* 80 (March 1970):

This assumption and the empirical evidence that supports it does not necessarily imply that skill requirements are identical for the same industries among countries. This would be the case if factor price equalization occurred, but no one expects this result under real world conditions. Instead one expects that the country with the

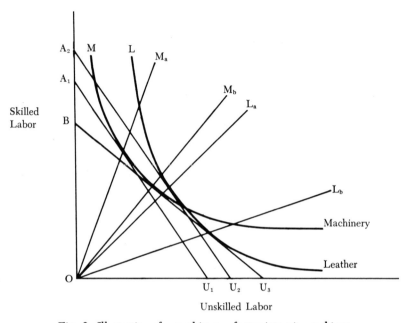

Fig. 2. Illustration of unambiguous factor-intensity rankings

relatively abundant endowment of skilled labor would have higher skill requirements for all industries than a country whose relatively abundant factor of production is unskilled labor. This proposition can be clarified by the familiar isoquant diagram. Figure 2 illustrates the two-country, two-factor, two-industry case. The factors of production are skilled labor and unskilled labor and the industries are the skill intensive machinery industry and the unskilled intensive leather industry. Country A is assumed to be relatively abundant in skilled labor on a price definition and country B is relatively abundant in unskilled labor. The slopes of the isocost

90. Actually, the similarity of rankings of earnings is presumptive rather than conclusive evidence for the assumptions of no factor intensity reversals due to the reason outlined in note 13.

lines reflect this assumption with isocost lines for country A, A_1U_1 and A_2U_2, showing a lower cost for skilled labor relative to the isocost line for country B, BU_3. The isoquants for machinery and leather are drawn under the assumption of linear homogeneous production functions in both industries and intersect only once, preventing the possibility of factor intensity reversals. The expansion paths are then drawn from the origin through the tangency points of the isocost and isoquant lines. The expansion paths also show the factor proportions of the four cases and illustrate that rankings by skill intensity are identical in the two countries and that the industries in the skill abundant country are all skill intensive relative to the same industries in the unskill abundant country.

Now for these findings to occur together in the n industry case, the industries in the skill abundant country must differ in skill intensity from the industries in the unskill abundant country only by a factor that does not disturb the order of the rankings. That is to say, the scale is unique up to a monotonic transformation. The more this principle is violated, the less likely that international comparisons of rankings by industry wage rates would be correlated. Indeed, the high correlations that have been found imply that the elasticity of substitution between skilled and unskilled labor does not vary significantly among manufacturing industries. If it did, factor intensity reversals would certainly occur. However, the elasticity of substitution as normally formulated depends upon the relative prices of the factors of production, i.e.:

$$(2) \qquad E_i^w = - \left[\frac{d\left(\dfrac{q_{i1}}{q_{i2}}\right)}{\dfrac{q_{i1}}{q_{i2}}} \div \frac{d\left(\dfrac{w_1}{w_2}\right)}{\dfrac{w_1}{w_2}} \right]$$

where E_i^w is the elasticity of substitution between factors as the relative wage rate between skilled labor, w_1, and unskilled labor, w_2, changes and the other symbols are as defined above. The evidence of similar rankings of industries implies that

$$(3) \qquad E_i^w = -K$$

for all industries $i = 1, 2, 3, \ldots m$ in a given country where $-K$ is some constant.

Actually, we need to know the elasticity of substitution as factor endowments vary on a quantity definition rather than a price definition, i.e.:

$$(4) \qquad E_i^Q = \frac{d\left(\dfrac{q_{i1}}{q_{i2}}\right)}{\dfrac{q_{i1}}{q_{i2}}} \div \frac{d\left(\dfrac{Q_1}{Q_2}\right)}{\dfrac{Q_1}{Q_2}}$$

where E_i^q is the elasticity of substitution due to changes in factor endowments and Q_1 and Q_2 are the physical endowments of skilled and unskilled labor respectively. The two elasticities are related in a very simple fashion since the elasticity of factor wage rates with respect to a change in factor endowments when producing a given output is equal to -1, i.e.:

$$(5) \qquad E_{wQ} = - \left[\frac{d\left(\dfrac{w_1}{w_2}\right)}{\dfrac{w_1}{w_2}} \div \frac{d\left(\dfrac{Q_1}{Q_2}\right)}{\dfrac{Q_1}{Q_2}} \right] = -1.$$

Thus, the elasticity of substitution as factor endowments vary is equal to the constant K. This follows since

$$(6) \qquad E_i^Q = E_i^w \cdot E_{wQ} = -K \ (-1) = K.$$

This means that all the industries of a skill abundant country will differ in skill intensity from the corresponding industries in the less skill abundant country by the factor, K, times the increase in the skill endowment ratio of the skill abundant country over the less skill abundant country, $d\left(\dfrac{Q_1}{Q_2}\right)$. In other words:

$$(7) \qquad d\left(\frac{q_{i1}}{q_{i2}}\right) = K \cdot d\left(\frac{Q_1}{Q_2}\right).$$

Thus, the Keesing version of the Heckscher-Ohlin theory as well as recent empirical evidence implies that the skill intensities of the industries of one country are likely to differ by a constant from the skill intensities of the corresponding industries of another country. In terms of equation (1) for the two-factor case, the W_i's (the industry wage rates) for a given country would differ from the W_i's of another country by the constant given by the right side of equation (7). The inter-industry wage structure would then certainly be a good proxy for the inter-occupational wage structure according to the Heckscher-Ohlin assumptions. However, the variation of occupational wages for different countries is of interest here, since this would be a comprehensive index of relative skill endowments on the price definition. The coefficient of variation for the occupational wage structure is defined as

$$(8) \qquad V_o = \frac{s}{\overline{w}} \quad \text{where } s = \sqrt{\frac{\sum_{j=1}^{n} (w_j - \overline{w})^2}{n}}$$

and $\overline{w}$ is the mean occupational wage. However, as shown above, the wage rates of the industries in a given country will differ from the corresponding industries in another country by the constant, K. Thus, the inter-industry coefficient of variation (V_i) will be a biased estimator of the inter-occupational coefficient of variation (V_o) in the following manner:

$$(9) \qquad V_i = \frac{s}{\overline{W}} = \frac{s}{\overline{w} + K \cdot d\left(\dfrac{Q_1}{Q_2}\right)}.$$

As the expression $d\left(\dfrac{Q_1}{Q_2}\right)$ goes from 0 for the least skill abundant

country to a maximum for the most skill abundant country, the inter-industry coefficient of variation will be increasingly understated. The standard deviation s is not affected by the addition of a constant because:

$$(10) \qquad s = \sqrt{\frac{\sum_{j=1}^{n}[(w_j + k) - (\overline{w} + k)]^2}{n}} = \sqrt{\frac{\sum_{j=1}^{n} (w_j - \overline{w})^2}{n}}.$$

The use of the inter-industry coefficient of variation as a proxy for the inter-occupational coefficient of variation thus appears to be a downward biased estimator for skill abundant countries under plausible assumptions.

TABLE 22.—COEFFICIENTS OF VARIATION FOR INTER-INDUSTRY WAGE STRUCTURES OF 17 COUNTRIES

	1965	1960	1955	1948
Hungary	7.4137	7.5697	10.6674	
West Germany	7.9759	10.2090	11.1931	9.2988
Sweden	8.6726	8.0370	9.0709	8.4030
United Kingdom	9.0088	8.4714	6.3944	6.0487
East Germany	10.8626	6.6717	15.6693	
India	13.2486	19.9821	24.5350	17.1864
Poland	14.1076	14.9663	17.2461	
France	16.6954	18.2756	12.9111	11.4096
Taiwan	17.7116	18.1340	24.6292	28.6005
United States	17.8241	18.2011	17.1651	14.2907
United Arab Republic	18.5234	24.5536	40.3973	37.6183
Costa Rica	19.8309	17.7348	17.6231	
Japan	23.0550	28.5103	25.8530	26.5183
Burma	23.5646	22.2260	43.3767	
Mexico	28.6115	29.0796	29.2500	22.1622
Ghana	34.7196	33.8220	41.2797	
Kenya	44.9866	26.9102	19.2983	

SOURCE: Papola and Bharadwaj, "Dynamics of Industrial Wage Structure," Table I, p. 76.
NOTE: The trend in the coefficients of variation is discussed in chapter 5.

This is an important finding in light of the recent study by Papola and Bharadwaj which estimates coefficients of variation (or dispersion) of industrial wage rates for a large number of countries. Their study, according to the authors, is the widest examination in terms of number of countries and time period that has yet been attempted in a study of the inter-industry wage structure (p. 74). It covered manufacturing industries in the two-digit "International Standard Classification of All Economic Activities" (ISIC) as given in the *Year Book of Labour Statistics* (ILO). Table 22 reproduces their results in calculating the coefficient of variation for 1965, 1960, 1955, and 1948 for the seventeen countries for which they were able to find data.

The results are quite startling. The United States' coefficient of variation in 1965 was 17.8241, which is closer to the bottom than the top in a ranking of lowest coefficients first. Such countries as West

Germany, Sweden, United Kingdom, France, and even India and Taiwan appear to have a greater relative abundance of skilled labor than the United States. The only important trading partners of the United States with higher coefficients of variation are Japan and Mexico.[16] When it is recalled that this United States coefficient of variation as an estimate of human capital abundance is biased downward relative to all the other countries on the list except Sweden, the conclusion unmistakably emerges that the United States' comparative advantage cannot lie, according to Heckscher-Ohlin reasoning, in skill intensive products. This is not to deny that its advantage lies in skill intensive products (because we have shown in chapter 3 that it does) but only that the Heckscher-Ohlin-Keesing theory does not logically predict this result. Skilled labor evidently is not the United States' relatively abundant factor of production on a price definition. The product cycle theory thus gains new support because it was shown in chapter 3 that the association between skill intensiveness and comparative advantage can also be explained by this approach.

An International Comparison of Distribution of Earnings

Inasmuch as this finding, that the United States' relatively abundant factor of production is not human capital, has such strong implications for modern orthodox trade theory, there is need for further evidence on this point. Lydall has just completed an extremely thorough theoretical and empirical investigation utilizing international data into the structure of earnings.[17] His main concern is distribution theory but he has gathered, he says, all the available empirical evidence that pertains to the distribution of employment income.[18] His method was to measure the dispersion of the "standard distribution" of as many countries as data restraints allowed.

16. For all intents and purposes the countries in Table 22 carry on most of the trade in manufactures in the world. Seven of the seventeen countries (the United States, Germany, the United Kingdom, France, Japan, Sweden, and India) together had almost 77 per cent of the share of world exports in 1959, according to Alfred Maizils, *Growth and Trade* (Cambridge: At the University Press, 1970), Table 81, p. 189. And of the seven, only Japan with 6.6 per cent of the world exports had a coefficient of variation in 1965 higher than the United States.

17. *The Structure of Earnings.*

18. Ibid., p. 137. Lydall states: "A systematic search has been made for information [on the distribution of employment income] from all countries, and it is believed that virtually all available sources have been covered."

Lydall defines the "standard distribution" as "Male adults, in all occupations, in all industries except farming, in all areas, working full-time and for the full period. The income measured should be money wages and salaries only, and before tax."[19]

The "standard distribution" is not the same thing as the inter-industry distribution. It differs by excluding females and including workers in non-manufacturing industries except for farming, and the level of aggregation is male adults rather than two-digit average industry wages. Lydall does not attempt to calculate the coefficient of variation. He argues that a single coefficient does not give one enough information on the shape of a distribution and that, therefore, several coefficients are needed.[20] The measure of dispersion that Lydall chooses is the quantile method defined from the top of the distribution as

$$(11) \qquad P_i = \frac{100p_i}{p_{50}} \ ;$$

$i = 5, 10, 50, 75$ where p_{50} is the median and p_5, for example, is the average earnings of the top 5 per cent of the income distribution. P_5 would, therefore, be the average income of the top 5 per cent of the population as a percentage of the median income. The average earnings of the income class p_i depend upon the average skill content (human capital) of p_i and the earnings associated with this level of skill content. The higher the skill content, the higher the average earnings will be. The earnings associated with a given skill class will depend upon the skill endowment on the supply side and on the derived demands for skills on the demand side.

In calculating P_i, $100p_i$ is divided by p_{50}, the median earnings of the population which also will depend on the skill content of

---

19. Ibid., p. 60. The reason for the exclusion of fringe benefits, according to Lydall, is that there is very little evidence on the international distribution of fringe benefits. However, Lydall feels that their addition would increase the dispersion of the distribution of earnings of all non-agricultural workers, especially in the richer countries, since fringe benefits are relatively more important at higher income levels. The view that fringe benefits are more important in developed countries is diametrically opposed to Fuchs' view on the subject (see chap. 1n30). If Lydall is correct, then the "standard distribution" will present a lower limit to the variation of earnings in the higher per capita income countries, a bias similar to the one expected for the inter-industry variation.

20. Ibid., p. 138. Lydall also favors this measure over the coefficient of variation due to data limitations.

this segment of the population. A country heavily endowed with human capital would tend to have a more highly skilled top 5 per cent as well as median population. Thus, the assumption will be made that the skill content effect on P_i is negligible or randomly distributed among countries.[21] This allows us to attribute variations in P_i as mainly determined by relative wage rates which, of course, on the supply side do depend on relative human capital endowments. Thus, P_i is an estimate of the relative abundance of skilled labor and is the empirical evidence that we wish to examine.

Table 23 reproduces Lydall's dispersion measures for the twenty-five countries for which data were available. The United States again appears in the middle of the ranking. The additional non-Communist countries, not found in the Papola and Bharadwaj study, which seem to have more abundant endowments of skilled labor on a price definition than the United States are New Zealand, Australia, Denmark, Canada, and Belgium. Since we have used the coefficient of variation statistics for the seventeen-country Papola and Bharadwaj study and the P_5 coefficient for the twenty-five-country Lydall study both as proxies for a measure of dispersion for earnings by skill class, the two sets of estimates should be highly correlated if they are measuring the same thing. A Spearman rank correlation coefficient was, therefore, calculated for the ten countries common to both sets.[22] The correlation coefficient was +.945, which is significant at the .01 level. This reinforces our confidence in the two measures. It also appears that both measures seem to be understating the dispersion of high income countries to the same degree.

THE EVIDENCE FROM SKILL-DIFFERENTIALS

There are available a few direct estimates of the relative costs of labor by skill levels. These measures or skill differentials have been used mainly to indicate changes in the relative price of labor over time and there are few international comparisons, the reason being

21. This assumption is consistent with the assumption previously made, that all industries of a skill abundant country are uniformly more skill intensive; this is a "conservative" assumption since the skill levels of the top 5 per cent of the population are not likely to differ as much between two countries as the skill levels of their median populations.

22. The ten countries were Hungary, West Germany, Sweden, the United Kingdom, India, Poland, France, the United States, Japan, and Mexico.

that there is considerable difficulty in finding pairs of skilled jobs and unskilled jobs that mean the same in a large number of countries whose wages or earnings are in comparable international terms. Where these calculations have been made, they are usually for manual workers paid wages, not salary, and, therefore, not as

TABLE 23.—APPROXIMATE RANK ORDER OF COUNTRIES BY DEGREE OF DISPERSION

COUNTRY AND YEAR	PERCENTILES OF STANDARD DISTRIBUTION		
	P5	P10	P75
Czechoslovakia, 1964	165	145	85
New Zealand, 1960–61	178	150	83
Hungary, 1964	180	155	83
Australia, 1959–60	185	157	84
Denmark, 1956	200	160	82
United Kingdom, 1960–61	200	162	80
Sweden, 1959	200	165	78
Yugoslavia, 1963	200	166	80
Poland	200	170	76
Germany (F.R.), 1957	205	165	77
Canada, 1960–61	205	166	79
Belgium, 1964	206	164	82
United States, 1959	206	167	75
Austria, 1957	210	170	80
Netherlands, 1959	215	175	70
Argentina, 1961	215	175	75
Spain, 1964	220	180	75
Finland, 1960	250	200	73
France, 1963	280	205	73
Japan, 1955	270	211	64
Brazil, 1953	380	250	
India, 1958–59	400	300	65
Ceylon, 1963	400	300	
Chile, 1964	400	300	
Mexico, 1960	450	280	65

SOURCE: Lydall, The Structure of Earnings, Table 5.5, p. 153.

highly skilled as we would like for this study. However, the evidence that is available does support our findings that the United States is not relatively well endowed with skilled labor on a price definition.

One of the first studies was by John Dunlop and Melvin Rothbaum.[23] They calculated the percentage by which the "skilled wage" exceeded the "unskilled wage" in three countries, and their results appear in Table 24. They conclude that "the range of inter-industry

TABLE 24.—Percentage by Which the Skilled Wage Exceeds the Unskilled Wage

	1937–40 (per cent)	1952–53 (per cent)
Italy	54	25
France	30	23
United States	65	37

Source: Dunlop and Rothbaum, "International Comparisons of Wage Structures," p. 356.

TABLE 25.—An International Comparison of Skill Differentials: Common Laborers as a Percentage of Bricklayers

Country	S.D. (per cent)	Country	S.D. (per cent)	Country	S.D. (per cent)
Sweden	94	Ceylon	83	Spain	75
Australia	91	Denmark	82	Argentina	74
Belgium	90	Austria	82	United States	72
New Zealand	89	Germany (F.R.)	76	Mexico	68
Finland	88	Hungary	75	Japan	65
United Kingdom	87	Netherlands	75	Canada	63

Source: Lydall, The Structure of Earnings, Table 5.5, p. 153.

wage differential varies considerably among the countries. The United States shows larger percentage differences than either Italy or France" (p. 358).

Lydall computed skill differentials from a wage survey, undertaken by the International Labor Organization, which expresses the hourly wage rates in 1964 for adult laborers in building expressed as a percentage of rates for bricklayers. These results appear in Table 25. The United States is fifteenth among eighteen countries. Only in Canada, Japan, and Mexico do bricklayers receive relatively higher wages than common laborers in comparison with the United States. This is even stronger evidence than that presented by the two dispersion studies that the United States is relatively abundant in unskilled labor. However, this index is more apt to be influenced by individual aberrations in labor market conditions and so is less reliable than the first two measures.

Thus, skilled labor appears to be relatively more scarce in the United States than in most other developed nations in the West. Even some underdeveloped nations seem to have a greater abun-

23. "International Comparisons of Wage Structures," International Labor Review 70 (April 1955): 356.

dance of skilled labor than the United States, as evidenced by the fact that India, Taiwan, Argentina, and Ceylon have appeared in various studies above the United States in measures of skill abundance. Actually, this evidence, although revolutionary in terms of the Heckscher-Ohlin-Keesing approach to international trade, has not been completely unknown to several well-known labor economists. Walter Galenson, in summarizing a volume of papers on the labor markets of several developing economies, reports the surprising results (to the authors) that "For one reason or another, narrow rather than wide wage differentials seem to prevail in underdeveloped countries. In Pakistan, the skilled-unskilled ratio is about two to one, roughly the United States' ratio a quarter of a century ago. The premium for skill in Indonesia is only about 50 per cent, while Israel has one of the most compressed wage and salary structures in the world."[24] Galenson claims that other variables in addition to supply and demand, namely sociological factors, are responsible for this "uneconomic state of affairs" (p. 8).

EVIDENCE FROM INTERNATIONAL MIGRATION OF HUMAN CAPITAL

The final type of evidence that has been drawn upon to test the hypothesis that the United States' relatively abundant factor of production is human capital has to do with factor movements. According to the Heckscher-Ohlin-Keesing theory, the United States' relatively abundant factor of production, skilled labor, should be migrating to countries where skilled labor is scarce and, therefore, earning a higher relative and absolute rate of return. Furthermore, unskilled labor should be migrating to the United States where, according to the Heckscher-Ohlin-Keesing assumptions, it not only receives a relatively higher wage but also an absolutely higher wage. This follows from the law of variable proportions since the Heckscher-Ohlin-Keesing theory holds that physical capital is highly mobile, and, thus, about evenly spread out, at least among the developed countries of the world. The theory also rules out differing technologies and economies of scale. The United States under these assumptions can still have the highest per capita income in the world since it also has the highest per capita endowment of human capital.

Reality seems to belie these predictions. Factor movements are

24. Galenson, ed., *Labor in Developing Economies* (Berkeley: University of California Press, 1962), p. 8.

in the opposite direction, and few would hold that the absolute wage rate of unskilled workers is lower in the United States than in the rest of the world. The literature and the empirical evidence on the so-called brain drain is another indication that skilled labor is relatively scarce in the United States. A chronological reading of the literature on the brain drain reveals a growing realization that, in the words of one writer, the drain is the result of an "overflow," or push factors, as well as pull factors.[25]

From a strong concern in the early sixties on the part of the countries of origin, especially the developing countries,[26] and even a concern on the part of the United States[27] that this international flow of human capital was having harmful effects on the country of origin, recent attention has turned to the beneficial effects of this factor movement on both the sending and receiving countries.[28] The reason for this change, as Baldwin put it, is that "The less developed countries (LDC's) are not being stripped of manpower they badly need; more often than not they are being relieved of manpower they cannot use" (p. 359). He then cites bits of evidence on the shortage or surplus of skilled manpower for the LDC's in five developing areas, East and Southeast Asia, India, East Africa, the Middle East, and Latin America, and concludes that "Since all countries are equally exposed to United States influences, this differential impact suggests that the main explanation for high losses must be attributable primarily to conditions in those countries" (p. 367).

Another writer, Alice W. Shurcliff, is also concerned with the

25. George B. Baldwin, "Brain Drain or Overflow?" *Foreign Affairs* 48 (January 1970): 358. On this point see also Subbiah Kannappan, "The Brain Drain and Developing Countries," *International Labor Review* 98 (July 1968): 1–26, and Hla Myint, "The Underdeveloped Countries: A Less Alarmist View," in *The Brain Drain*, ed. Walter Adams (New York: The Macmillan Company, 1968), pp. 233–46. It will be stressed later that the push factors are caused by the structure of aggregate demand, not its size.

26. For example, see Brinley Thomas, "The International Circulation of Human Capital," *Minerva* 5, no. 4 (Summer 1967): 479–506; James A. Wilson, "The Emigration of British Scientists," *Minerva* 5, no. 1 (Autumn 1966): 21–28; and George Coutsoumaris, "Greece," in *The Brain Drain*, pp. 166–82.

27. This is illustrated by two publications of the House of Representatives, Committee on Government Operations: *The Brain Drain into the United States of Scientists, Engineers, and Physicians* (90th Cong., 1st sess., Staff Study for the Research and Technical Programs Subcommittee, 1967), and *The Brain Drain of Scientists, Engineers, and Physicians from the Developing Countries into the United States, Hearings* (90th Cong., 2d sess., 1968).

28. The authors of the articles listed in note 25 support this contention.

problem of too many educated graduates in many LDC's,[29] and presents the following evidence to illustrate her concern. The increase

TABLE 26.—ANNUAL PERCENTAGE RATE OF INCREASE OF GNP AND
UNIVERSITY GRADUATES, 1960–65

	GNP	UNIVERSITY GRADUATES
Israel	6%	27%
Philippines	4	12
India	3	8
Taiwan	10	10
United States	4	4
Turkey	4	4
Puerto Rico	10	8
Japan	11	7

SOURCE: Shurcliff, "Manipulating Demand and Supply of High-level Manpower."

in GNP is a proxy for the demand for human capital while the increase in university graduates is the supply of human capital. The difference is taken by Shurcliff as an approximation for the disequilibrium and brings out the point that skill differentials are not a simple function of a country's level of economic development. A country's educational system can be quite independent from demand factors. A point not brought out by this table is that the structure of demand and the mix of aggregate supply of human capital could be as important as the disequilibrium between aggregate demand and supply. The result of these disequilibriums is, given some degree of factor mobility, an outflow or inflow of human capital. Baldwin lists Israel, the Philippines, India, and Taiwan as countries with heavy outflows of human capital, and Japan as having no outflow problems (pp. 364–66).

Kannappan, in an article which emphasizes India's problem of too much human capital, puts the problem in perspective. Two statements express his view quite clearly: "As a general proposition one may suppose that the more poorly developed a country is, the more limited its demand is likely to be for educated manpower characterised by a high degree of specialization or advanced technical or scientific accomplishments" and "But assuming that the distribution of abilities pertinent to educational attainment is random among different population groups, it is not surprising that the edu-

29. "Manipulating Demand and Supply of High-level Manpower," *International Labor Review* 101, no. 2 (February 1970): 133–47.

cational levels actually attained by individuals sometimes diverge from the domestic demand for these attainments."[30]

The misconception that developed countries are relatively abundant in skilled labor and that developing countries are relatively scarce in skilled labor seems to have been due to a one-sided view of the problem.[31] The demand side as well as the supply side determines the relative scarcity of human capital. And since both the demand and supply of human capital increase with development, one cannot determine a priori the relative scarcity of a country's human capital endowment by just knowing its stage of development. Shifts in the supply curve due to the deliberate educational policies of development planners frequently are more important than shifts in the demand curve.[32] Thus, the flow of skilled manpower to the United States and the relative scarcity of human capital in the United States are not as paradoxical as they seem.

To put the magnitude of the phenomenon into perspective, a few statistics seem in order. The size of the flow to the United States is quite large. From 1947 to 1965, Brinley Thomas has estimated, 372,-204 out of 2,208,405 immigrants to the United States were professional and technical workers (p. 482). In the last year of the estimate, 22.0 per cent of the total were professional and technical workers, up from an average of 16.9 per cent for the whole period. Table 27 breaks down the immigration of scientists and engineers for the period 1949–66 into more detail, showing country of origin for the period 1956–66.

In the beginning of this chapter, it was pointed out that with only a single exception the human capital trade theorists have neglected to mention these perverse (to them) factor movements.

30. Kannappan, p. 16. Note that, *ceteris paribus*, the two quotes taken together imply that in developing countries skilled labor will be more abundant on a price definition than unskilled labor.

31. Lydall, for one, concludes that supply side factors are the sole determinants of the long-term dispersion of earnings and that education policy, which he says is determined by social factors, is the main factor (pp. 254–66). Also note Yahr's assumption, "I also postulate that, since one scarce factor in an underdeveloped country is skilled labor, those countries will specialize in industries requiring relatively less skilled labor" (p. 93).

32. India in the postwar period provides a good example of this occurrence. A. M. Nalla Gounden, "Investment in Education in India," *Journal of Human Resources* 2 (Summer 1967): 347–58, has calculated that India's educational expenditure as a percentage of national income increased from 1.2 in 1950 to 2.9 in 1965, with the result that the internal rate of return to education is lower than to physical capital at all levels of schooling except primary.

TABLE 27.—Immigration of Scientists and Engineers to the United States and Country of Last Residence, 1949–66

	1949	1950	1951	1952	1953	1954	1955
Total	1,234	1,519	1,561	2,297	2,718	3,200	2,862

	1956	1957	1958	1959	1960	1961	1962	1963	1964	1965	1966
Total	3,918	5,823	5,190	5,081	4,326	3,922	4,297	5,933	5,762	5,345	7,114
Europe	1,733	2,958	2,171	2,412	1,916	1,608	1,764	2,318	2,982	2,978	2,830
Germany	357	659	423	428	324	291	303	376	491	449	363
United Kingdom	440	842	790	485	614	575	688	939	1,175	1,194	1,283
Canada	1,020	444	1,193	1,257	1,265	1,040	1,195	1,221	685	762	1,167
Mexico	132	61	62	45	64	54	76	90	55	67	98
South America	330	450	500	340	360	349	368	485	426	384	408
Asia	296	431	644	640	350	336	344	1,305	1,053	566	1,907
Other	417	401	436	372	280	364	394	427	561	588	704

Sources: 1949–55 from H. G. Grubel and A. D. Scott, "Immigration of Scientists and Engineers to the United States, 1949–1961," Journal of Political Economy 74, no. 4 (August 1966): 368–69; 1957–61 from National Science Foundation, Scientific Manpower from Abroad (Washington: U.S. Government Printing Office, 1962); 1962–65 from National Science Foundation, "Scientists and Engineers from Abroad," Review Data Science Resources 1, no. 5 (July 1965): 5–7; 1956 and 1966 from Committee on Government Operations, The Brain Drain into the United States of Scientists, Engineers, and Physicians, Tables I and VI.

The single exception was Ball, who thought this paradox could be resolved by the fact that the United States had a higher absolute wage level due to its more abundant supply of "both tangible capital and skilled labor, and doubtless for other reasons as well."[33] And it was also pointed out above that these reasons are all inconsistent with the factor proportions theory. However, Ball further states that "The absolute difference between U.S. and foreign wages in the lower skill levels is also large, but both U.S. immigration policy and the relatively greater difficulties of securing U.S. employment in advance and financing a trip severely reduce the migration of unskilled labor to the U.S."[34] Perhaps the factor flow does not contradict the assumption of United States human capital abundance after all. Let us examine Ball's three points: the costs of securing employment, the cost of financing the trip, and United States immigration policy. The first point, that the uncertainty or the costs of securing employment are greater for the unskilled than for the skilled worker, actually tends to support the contention that the excess demand for skilled workers is greater than the excess demand for unskilled workers in the United States, and, therefore, the costs of securing employment are lower for skilled workers. This is illustrated by the lower unemployment rates for skilled workers relative to unskilled workers in the United States.[35] This directly reduces the uncertainty of finding a job and is a direct measure of relative excess demand for skilled labor. Note that it is not always true that unemployment rates decrease with education level. The opposite is the case in India.[36] However, given similar unemployment rates, it can be argued that the more highly specialized a worker, the lower the direct costs of job search to the potential employee (and the higher for the employer) are likely to be.[37]

33. See chap. 4n4.
34. "Studies in the Basis of International Trade," p. 73. Note that Ball makes the implicit assumption that workers do not migrate unless they have secured employment "in advance."
35. The unemployment rates in 1965 in the United States ranged from 1.5 per cent for professional and technical workers, to 3.6 per cent for craftsmen and foremen, to 8.6 per cent for non-farm laborers (Dept. of Labor, *Manpower Report of the President* [Washington, 1970], Table A.2, p. 232).
36. Gounden, p. 358.
37. The more specialized a worker, the more likely that the employer will undertake the job search. The costs of job search will be less for the employee because, as a worker becomes more specialized, the probability that a given worker will accept a job offer is greater relative to the probability that a given

Second, the monetary cost of the trip should be a minor factor when one considers that the motivating factor should be the present value of the increased expected future stream of income or the increase in permanent income. A rational rule for migration would be

$$(12) \qquad \sum_{i=1}^{N} \frac{Y_i^{us}}{(1+r)^i} > \sum_{i=1}^{N} \frac{Y_i^{o}}{(1+r)^i} - C$$

where Y is real income, N is the expected number of years of work left, C is the costs of the trip, r is the emigrant's rate of discount, us is the superscript standing for the United States, and o is the superscript standing for the country of origin. This means that a trip cost of $1,000 would be overcome by an income stream of $94.39 more a year in the United States than in the country of origin, assuming a rate of discount of 7 per cent, an expected work life of twenty years, and the fact that psychic income is the same in both countries.[38]

The third point, that United States immigration laws tend to discriminate in favor of skilled workers, can be examined empirically. S. Watanabe has calculated the percentage of professional, technical, and kindred workers that used the occupational preference quota to immigrate to the United States as 7.4 per cent in 1962, 14.5 per cent in 1963, 8.9 per cent in 1964, 5.1 per cent in 1965, and 15.1 per cent in 1966.[39] Another way to look at it is that in 1964 only a little over 2 per cent of the 292,248 immigrants of all categories admitted to the United States used the special skill quota.[40]

---

employer needs additional workers. See George J. Stigler, "Information in the Labor Market," *Journal of Political Economy* 70 Supplement (October 1962): 101–2.

38. The $94.39 was calculated by dividing $1,000 by the present value of a one dollar annuity for twenty years at 7 per cent. This example, of course, assumes either that the unskilled workers have the $1,000 available or that capital markets are relatively well functioning.

39. "The Brain Drain from Developing to Developed Countries," *International Labor Review* 99, no. 4 (April 1969): 423.

40. Bureau of the Census, *Statistical Abstract of the United States* (Washington, 1965), Table 126, p. 47. Most skilled workers, therefore, did not need to use the skill preference quota to gain entry to the United States. This is because many could gain entry through the familial relationship quota, and because the national origin quotas were frequently unfilled. This was especially true for Canada, which has no quota, and for the United Kingdom and Ger-

Therefore, Ball's complicated explanation of the paradox is open to question, and it seems safe to conclude that although the reasons mentioned by Ball may have some validity, they do not appear strong enough alone to explain the tremendous flow of human capital into the United States as documented in Table 27. The simple explanation for the large influx of scientists and engineers into the United States in the postwar period is that there was a relative shortage of skilled labor in the United States as manifested by the higher relative and absolute wages and salaries for human capital in the United States.[41]

All four types of evidence, the inter-industry variation of wages, the distribution of earnings, the skill differentials, and the factor flows, are consistent with each other and point to the conclusion that at least from 1950 to 1965, the United States did not have a relative abundance of skilled labor on the price definition. Some other explanation for the skill intensity of United States exports is needed. However, before we conclude that demand reversals reduce the usefulness of the Heckscher-Ohlin-Keesing theory, let us put these findings in perspective.

CONCLUSIONS AND FURTHER INVESTIGATIONS

First, these conclusions hold only for a given period and time and for one country, although admittedly this is a long period of time and the country has the largest share of exports of manufactures in the world. Second, the alternative theory, the product cycle theory, has mainly been proposed and empirically supported for the case of the United States' trade pattern. Therefore, using data that we have already developed, let us test the validity of the Heckscher-Ohlin-Keesing theory for as many other countries as our data permit.

It will be recalled that a high association was found between physical endowments of skilled labor and skill intensity of exports

---

many, which have very large national origin quotas and supply on the average one-half of all the scientists and engineers admitted to the United States.

41. The evidence on relative wages has been presented above. On the absolute wage differential, note this conclusion of Adams: "According to the British Government's Working Party on Migration, the starting salaries in most professional categories are three times higher in the United States than in Great Britain. Other estimates, depending on the country involved, confirm the existence of a wide differential. And, this differential is an inevitable magnet for migration" (p. 248).

as estimated by Keesing, using United States skill requirements.[42] This is strong support for the Keesing theory for a large number of important trading nations. The difficulty was that for the United States, the physical abundance of skilled labor became a scarcity on a price definition, due evidently to a strong domestic demand for skill intensive products. The validity of this test, and, therefore, the quantity definition approach, rests on the extent of the demand reversals phenomenon. This can be checked by calculating Spearman coefficients comparing the rankings of a set of countries on the physical definition of skill abundance against their rankings on the price definition of skill abundance. From Tables 20 and 22 the eleven countries common to both rankings were selected, and a Spearman coefficient of +.514, which is not quite significant at the .05 level, was calculated.[43] Besides the United States, two other countries, France and Mexico, underwent what might be called demand reversals of their physical skill abundance. All three countries dropped three places on the price skill abundance scale relative to the quantity skill abundance scale. The demand reversal phenomenon, therefore, does pose some problems for the factor proportions theory using the quantity definition.

Thus, a test of the Heckscher-Ohlin theory, using price definitions of skill abundance, seems in order. From Tables 21 and 22, a Spearman coefficient was calculated for the seven common countries showing the relationship between skill intensity of exports and the inter-industry coefficient of variation for 1960.[44] The coefficient was +.653, which is not significant at the .05 level. However, if the United States is dropped from the list, the coefficient rises to +.867, which is significant at the .05 level. As a check, the second method of measuring relative skill abundance, the Lydall dispersion measure, was compared with the skill intensity of export index. From Table 21 and column p_5 of Table 23, the rankings of the eleven common countries were used to calculate a Spearman coefficient of +.720, which is significant at the .05 level.[45] However, when

42. See p. 75.
43. The eleven countries were the United States, Sweden, France, the United Kingdom, West Germany, Costa Rica, Japan, Mexico, Ghana, the United Arab Republic, and Taiwan.
44. The seven countries were the United States, Sweden, Germany, the United Kingdom, France, Japan, and India.
45. The eleven countries were the United States, Sweden, Germany, the United Kingdom, Canada, the Netherlands, France, Austria, Belgium, Japan, and India.

the United States is dropped from the group, the coefficient rises to +.764, which is significant at the .01 level. Thus, the Heckscher-Ohlin-Keesing theory, using the price definition, receives strong empirical support, especially when the United States is dropped from the sample. Thus, although this study has been mainly concerned with explanations of United States trade patterns, a major finding which has emerged is that the factor proportions theory does explain the trade patterns of other nations quite well. And, indeed, this is to be expected, since the product cycle theory as an explanation of United States trade patterns rests on the unique characteristics of the United States' economy, and, therefore, has not been proposed as a separate explanation of other nations' trade patterns.

Thus, the results of chapter 3 have been corroborated by a quite different approach. For the United States, the Heckscher-Ohlin-Keesing theory cannot logically claim to predict United States trade patterns, since the United States' relatively abundant factor of production under the price definition does not seem to be human capital. However, using the price definitions for other countries, the Keesing approach does receive strong support, and the two theories do appear to be complementary. Different theories seem to explain different countries' trade patterns.

5. The Causes and Implications of the United States' Demand Reversal in Human Capital

The phenomenon of a demand reversal for the United States and a few of the logical implications for United States comparative advantage and for the applicability of the product cycle and Heckscher-Ohlin theories will now be explored. Chapter 3 showed that the United States' relatively abundant factor of production on a quantity basis was human capital, but that on a price basis human capital did not appear to be relatively abundant. This phenomenon constitutes a demand reversal. Thus the United States' demand structure must be biased toward human capital intensive products relative to other countries. This causes the derived demand for human capital to be greater in the United States than in other countries, and even though the supply of human capital is also greater, its price is relatively higher in the United States than in many other countries. This situation is illustrated in Figure 3. The production possibility curves in the figure show that the United States has a comparative advantage in the production of the skill intensive good, machinery, due to its physical abundance of skilled labor. However, the United States' strong demand for the skilled labor intensive good, machinery, as illustrated by the community indifference curve I_{us}, offsets the United States' comparative advantage in the production of that good as shown by the United States' price of machinery in terms of leather, P_{us}, being greater than the price of machinery in terms of leather, P_{row}, for the rest of the world.[1]

---

1. The sufficient although not necessary conditions for the preclusion of demand reversals are that tastes in the two countries be identical and that the income elasticity of demand for each good be unity. See Subimal Mookerjee, *Factor Endowment and International Trade* (Bombay: Asia Publishing House, 1958), pp. 43–44. This in turn implies that the indifference maps are identical and that the indifference curves are homothetic. Therefore, the existence of a demand reversal means that these assumptions must have been violated.

Thus, the Heckscher-Ohlin theory predicts, contrary to fact, that the United States should not be exporting human capital intensive products. This is a new and startling conclusion, as it was previously thought that the labor skills or human capital approach to the Heckscher-Ohlin theory had saved that theory from the disillusionment that many economists felt toward it as a result of Leontief's

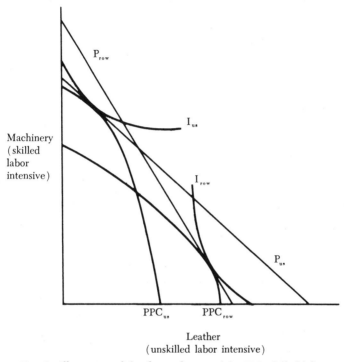

Fig. 3. Illustration of the demand reversal for U.S. skilled labor

study. It is interesting to note that a demand reversal argument also entered that controversy, but from a different direction. As an explanation for the Leontief Paradox, Robinson and Valavanis-Vail raised the specter of demand reversal for the United States' tangible capital intensive commodities.[2] Since trade patterns did

2. For criticisms of this view, see Robinson, "Factor Proportions and Comparative Advantage: Parts I and II," *Quarterly Journal of Economics* 70 (May and August 1956): 169–92, 346–63; Valavanis-Vail, "Leontief's Scarce Factor Paradox"; A. J. Brown, "Professor Leontief and the Pattern of World Trade," *Yorkshire Bulletin of Economics and Social Research* 9 (Nov. 1957): 63–75.

not seem to reflect a priori conceptions as to factor abundance, the factor abundance assumptions were modified. In the present case, trade patterns did seem to reflect the preconceptions of factor abundance, and, therefore, it evidently seemed unnecessary to conduct further investigations into the possibility of a demand reversal and into the empirical basis for factor abundance. I have attempted to rectify this lack of rigor on the part of previous studies.

TABLE 28.—RELATIVE CHANGE IN COEFFICIENT OF VARIATION FOR WAGE STRUCTURE IN 10 COUNTRIES, 1948–65

	COEFFI- CIENT OF VARIATION, 1948	COEFFI- CIENT OF VARIATION, 1965	RELATIVE CHANGE (per cent)
United Kingdom	6.05	9.01	50.0
France	11.41	16.70	46.5
Mexico	22.16	28.61	28.8
United States	14.30	17.82	24.5
Sweden	8.40	8.67	3.6
Japan	26.52	23.06	–12.8
West Germany	9.30	7.96	–14.0
India	17.19	13.25	–23.2
Taiwan	28.60	17.71	–38.1
United Arab Republic	37.62	18.52	–50.7

SOURCE: Calculated from Table 22.

It has been shown that a demand reversal for human capital exists in the United States. This leads to a few additional questions. Is this demand reversal unique to the United States and has it recently occurred, or is this the usual relationship between the price and quantity of human capital? To answer these questions conclusively we would need international data on relative wage rates going back at least as far as the turn of the century, but the available data go back only to 1948. The Papola and Bharadwaj data cited provide coefficients of variation for a sample of ten countries for the period 1948–65.[3] The relative change in the coefficients of variation has been calculated and appears as Table 28. Over this seventeen-year period the United States' coefficient of variation actually increased by 25.5 per cent, which places the United States fourth behind the United Kingdom, France, and Mexico in the magnitude of increase. Thus, over this period, there has been an increase in the price of skilled labor relative to unskilled labor in the

3. See Table 22.

United States.[4] The premium for skilled labor has increased in the United States relative to Sweden, West Germany, Japan, the United Arab Republic, Taiwan, and India over this period. There are two main explanations for the changes over time of inter-industry wage dispersion. M. W. Reder claims that declines in wage dispersion come about from shifts in the level of aggregate demand which affect hiring standards. When demand is strong, hiring standards are lowered and substitution of less skilled workers for more skilled workers takes place. According to Reder, this reduces the supply of unskilled workers and thus reduces wage differentials.[5] However, H. A. Turner believes that trade unions are the main cause of decreases in skill margins.[6] Unions are thought to demand equal wage increases for their members on the basis of equity considerations. Along with this argument one might add the effect of government interference with the wage structure through the enactment of minimum wage legislation.

These exogenous interferences may be particularly important in underdeveloped countries. In a study of Puerto Rico, Lloyd Reynolds found conclusively that minimum wage legislation is much more important in narrowing the wage structure there than it is in the United States, because most workers in each industry earn very close to the minimum rate.[7] The importance of minimum wage legislation in narrowing skill differentials in the lesser developed countries has also been noted by Koji Taira.[8]

4. It was argued in chapter 4 that the coefficient of variation was a proxy for relative price of skilled labor.
5. "The Theory of Occupational Wage Differentials," *American Economic Review* 44 (December 1955): 833–52, as reprinted in *The Labour Market*, eds. B. J. McCormick and E. Owen Smith (Baltimore: Penguin Books, 1968). Note that Reder's theory amounts to the assumption that the elasticity of supply is greater for skilled than for unskilled workers, and seems to neglect the evidence of wide variation in the participation rates of unskilled workers. For example, see Charles C. Killingsworth, "The Continuing Labor Market Twist," *Monthly Labor Review* 91 (September 1968): 12–17.
6. "Inflation and Wage Differentials in Great Britain," in *The Theory of Wage Determination*, ed. J. T. Dunlop (London: Macmillan, 1957), as reprinted in McCormick and Smith, eds., pp. 228–42.
7. "Wages and Employment in a Labor-Surplus Economy," *American Economic Review* 55 (March 1965): 19–39. Reynolds points out that this is true because in Puerto Rico minimum wage rates are frequently changed and different rates are set for each industry according to the wage-paying ability of each industry.
8. "Wage Differentials in Developing Countries: A Survey of Findings," *International Labour Review* 83 (March 1966): 281–301.

In the case of the sample countries in Table 28, this latter explanation may be quite important, especially for the United Arab Republic and India, because in both countries important programs of government regulation of minimum wages were enacted during this period.[9] Also note that in two rapidly growing nations, Japan and West Germany, wage dispersion declined, while in a slower growing nation, the United Kingdom, wage dispersion increased. These occurrences are both consistent with the Reder thesis. It will be proposed that the actual composition of aggregate demand may also be important in affecting wage dispersion, especially in the cases of the United States, France, and Mexico.

Table 28 also reveals that even in 1948, human capital was relatively more expensive in the United States than in Sweden, France, West Germany, and the United Kingdom. The actual demand reversal may have taken place prior to 1948 although it seems to have been intensifying since then. It also appears that in several other countries, demand reversals might also be occurring in the near future, or if they have already taken place, they might be intensifying in magnitude. To examine this proposition, it is necessary to recall that when the eleven countries common to both sets of countries for which human capital abundance on the physical definition and on the price definition were compared, three countries (the United States, France, and Mexico) were identified as having a relative scarcity of human capital on the price definition as compared to the quantity definition. These countries represent three of the top four countries in rate of change of their coefficients of variation as shown in Table 28. The United Kingdom, the exception, evidently did not undergo a demand reversal because at the beginning of the period, in 1948, it had by far the lowest priced human capital of any of the countries in the sample.

We have already shown that the United States' strong preference for skill intensive products did not prevent it from also being the major exporter of these products. Let us look at the two other countries that have been identified as undergoing demand reversals. We do not have data on the skill composition of Mexico's exports, but for France we have Keesing's estimates of the skill content of her exports. Table 29 has been calculated from Tables 20–22. It can be seen that France's rankings are identical on the Keesing skill

9. Papola and Bharadwaj, p. 78.

mix index of exports and factor abundance on a price definition; but when the Keesing skill mix index of exports is compared to the factor abundance ranking on a quantity definition, France is four places higher on the factor abundance index than on the Keesing index.[10] This means that France's strong consumption preference for skill intensive products adversely affects her ability to export skill intensive products. Evidently, the factors that overcome the United States' comparative disadvantage in the price of skilled

TABLE 29.—INTERNATIONAL RANKINGS OF EXPORT PERFORMANCE AND SKILL INTENSIVE PRODUCTS AND FACTOR ABUNDANCE ESTIMATES ON THE PRICE AND QUANTITY DEFINITIONS

	KEESING SKILL INDEX FOR EXPORTS, 1962	RANK-ING	COEFFI-CIENT OF VARIATION, 1960	RANK-ING	PROFESSIONAL, TECHNICAL, AND RELATED WORKERS IN MANUFACTUR-ING, 1960	RANK-ING
United States	.654	1	18.2	4	7.45	2
Sweden	.547	2	8.0	1	9.57	1
West Germany	.541	3	10.2	3	5.14	6
United Kingdom	.484	4	8.4	2	5.44	4
Canada	.467	5			5.26	5
Netherlands	.418	6			4.35	7
France	.370	7	18.3	5	7.26	3
Belgium	.323	8			3.02	8
Japan	.281	9	28.5	7	1.78	9
India	.084	10	20.0	6		
Hong Kong	.084	11			1.08	10

SOURCES: Tables 20–22.

labor are not operating in France. This is as the product cycle predicts, since it is an asymmetrical theory promulgated only for the United States.

We can conclude from this empirical evidence that demand reversals are not unique to the United States because at least two other countries in our sample have undergone them. However, the usual relationship seems to be for the price and quantity of human capital to vary inversely, which means that over time and with normal growth the supply curve of human capital tends to shift more than the demand curve.[11] For the United States, France, and

10. This represents 57 per cent of the unexplained variance in a Spearman coefficient correlation between the ten countries in this sample.

11. Actually the correlation coefficient for the eleven-country sample for the relationship between the relative price and quantity of skilled labor was +.514 which is not quite significant at the .05 level. See Table 28. However,

Mexico, the opposite seems to be the case, at least for the short run and in recent years. Explanations for these occurrences will be attempted later in the chapter.

With regard to the timing of the actual demand reversal for the United States, more evidence is needed. Reliable data on the United States' labor market for scientists and engineers have been generated back to 1929. Table 30 presents the ratios of median engineering salaries to the earnings of full-time manufacturing wage earners. It is clear that over the period as a whole there has been a large decline in the relative earnings of engineers. David Blank and George Stigler, who generated these figures, concluded, "Rela-

TABLE 30.—INDEX OF RATIO OF MEDIAN ENGINEERING SALARY TO EARNINGS PER FULL-TIME MANUFACTURING WAGE EARNER

YEAR	RATIO	YEAR	RATIO
1929	100.0	1949	70.8
1932	109.1	1950	67.6
1934	97.3	1951	65.4
1939	108.5	1952	66.8
19'3	76.0	1953	66.1
1946	83.1	1954	66.6

SOURCE: David M. Blank and George J. Stigler, *The Demand and Supply of Scientific Personnel* (New York: National Bureau of Economic Research, 1957), Table 11, p. 25.

tive to both the working population as a whole and the professions as a separate class, then, the record of earnings would suggest that up to at least 1955 there had been no shortage—in fact an increasingly ample supply—of engineers."[12] However, their own data in Table 30 reveal that the "ample supply" was beginning to turn into a shortage as the ratio began to creep up from its low point in 1951. Table 31 indicates this tendency more clearly. The percentage increases in salaries of engineering graduates and of research scientists were greater than those of all manufacturing wage earners and of other college graduates starting in the 1950–53 period. However, Blank and Stigler did not attach very much impor-

---

if Costa Rica is dropped from the sample the coefficient rises to $+.709$ which is significant at the .05 level. Also Papola and Bharadwaj, p. 90, conclude that "The relative wage structure tends to be wider in the less industrialized than in the highly industrialized countries."

12. *The Demand and Supply of Scientific Personnel* (New York: National Bureau of Economic Research, Inc., 1957), pp. 28–29.

tance to this reversal: "After the outbreak of the Korean War there was a minor increase in the relative salaries of engineers (and of other college trained workers), but this was hardly more than a minor crosscurrent in a tide" (p. 28). Of course, they had no way of knowing that this "minor crosscurrent" would last twenty years, a period twice as long as the previous "tide" of falling relative wages for scientists and engineers. However, they did discover the factor causing this crosscurrent, although evidently they thought that the factor would be only temporary: it was the autonomous increase in demand for skill intensive products on the part of the United States

TABLE 31.—Percentage Increase in Salaries and Earnings by Selected Occupations, Various Periods 1950–56

	1950–53	1950–54	1950–55	1950–56
1. College graduates, average starting salaries				
Engineering	25.0	32.8	38.9	51.5
Accounting	24.8	32.4	39.5	47.9
Sales	25.4	30.8	40.0	49.2
General business	24.8	32.5	39.8	48.7
All fields	24.1	31.8	39.2	49.4
2. Research scientists and engineers with bachelor degrees, new graduates	27.0	31.7	41.2	
3. All manufacturing wage earners, average earnings per full-time employee	22.8	24.9	31.8	

Source: Blank and Stigler, Table 14, p. 28.

government. In their words, "After some declines in 1949 and early 1950, salaries for young engineers and scientists rose substantially under the impact of the Korean defense program. The largest increase took place in 1952, when apparently the full impact of the research and development programs of the federal government was felt" (p. 27).

Kenneth Arrow and William Capron were able to use job vacancy data to spot the shortage in the supply of engineers and scientists in the early 1950s.[13] They also explained this by the increase in government demand. They point out that there was a 23.7 per cent increase in the number of scientists and engineers doing research

13. "Dynamic Shortages and Price Rises: The Engineer-Scientist Case," *Quarterly Journal of Economics* 73, no. 2 (May 1959): 297.

and development in 1951 and that 15,547 of this increase of 17,557 could be attributed directly to government contracts with private firms for research and development work (pp. 302–3).

W. Lee Hansen, developing his own data and using the internal rate of return to measure the relative scarcities of various professions, found that the internal rate of return was 20 per cent for engineering graduates versus 14 per cent for all male college graduates in 1939.[14] In 1949 the internal rate of return had fallen to 12 per cent for both groups, but by 1956 the return to engineering increased to 17 per cent while the return to all college graduates remained at 12 per cent. The 1959 figures were the same as those for 1956. Thus Hansen concluded, "On this basis, we can conclude that shortages of engineers clearly existed in 1939 and 1956 (continuing to 1959), given the rate of return differentials in favor of engineers, while no shortage or surplus existed in 1949, given the absence of a differential" (p. 212). Reliable earnings data from the Bureau of Labor Statistics bring us up to 1968. From 1961 to 1968, average salaries for engineers increased by 31 per cent, for chemists by 34.5 per cent, and for clerical workers by 27.7 per cent.[15] The increase in relative wages for scientists and engineers that began in the early 1950s continued at least to 1968.

From this survey of the labor market for scientists and engineers, we can conclude that a shortage of technical manpower existed in the United States from as early as the Korean War up to at least 1968. Between 1929 and 1949, there seems to be conflicting evidence from the various sources, but it does appear that the excess demand for scientists and engineers has undergone several fluctuations. We cannot date the exact timing of the demand reversal for human capital in the United States, but we can state that the demand reversal grew in strength from 1950 to 1968.

The apparent reason for this increase in the relative price of human capital was the increase in the federal government's research and development program with the advent of the Korean

14. "The Economics of Scientific and Engineering Manpower," *Journal of Human Resources* 2 (Spring 1967): 211: "The rate-of-return approach consists of finding that rate of discount which equates the present value of the costs (direct plus income foregone) of education required for entry into an occupation with the present value of the incremental earnings stream yielded by the education."

15. "National Survey of Professional, Administrative, Technical, and Clerical Pay," *Bulletin* 1617 (January 1969): 3.

War. Table 32 presents the historical record of the federal government's expenditures for research and development by department or agency. The table reveals that there was a 200-fold increase in R & D expenditures by the federal government from 1940 to 1964, and that the composition of the spending by department has changed. While in 1964 the Department of Defense, the National Aeronautics and Space Administration, and the Atomic Energy Commission accounted for almost 90 per cent of the spending, in 1940 the Department of Defense accounted for only 35.6 per cent of total spending. Agricultural R & D spending declined from 39.3 per cent to 1.2 per cent during this same period. The history of the involvement of the federal government in R & D has been summed up by Edwin Mansfield: "Although the role of the Federal government in science and technology expanded steadily during the period preceding 1940, it was World War II that resulted in the enormous Federal involvement in research and development. During the war, a close partnership was established by the government, industry, and universities, this partnership being built around the use of contracts to finance government research carried out by private firms and nonprofit institutions. After the war Federal R and D expenditures rose dramatically, and two great science-oriented agencies, AEC and NSF, were created. In 1957, after the launching of the Sputnik I, the organization of national science policy was extensively revamped and another important new scientific agency, NASA, was created."[16]

Cross-sectional data also reveal the special role that the United States government plays in the demand for skilled labor. Table 33 shows the sources of finance for R & D expenditures in eight countries. France leads the list with 78 per cent of her R & D spending financed by the government, with the United States in second place with 66 per cent and the rest of the countries ranging from Finland's 62 per cent to the Netherlands' 30 per cent. It will be recalled that France and the United States were identified as having undergone demand reversals for human capital and as having large positive increases in the coefficients of variation of their inter-industry wage structures. Also, J.-J. Servan-Schreiber makes the point that the "American challenge" to Europe has been fueled in part by the greater R & D effort of the United States relative to

16. *The Economics of Technological Change* (New York: W. W. Norton and Company, Inc., 1968), p. 203.

TABLE 32.—FEDERAL EXPENDITURES FOR RESEARCH AND DEVELOPMENT BY DEPARTMENT OR AGENCY FOR SELECTED FISCAL YEARS

	1940		1948		1956		1964	
	Millions	%	Millions	%	Millions	%	Millions	%
Agriculture	$29.1	39.3	$ 42.4	5.0	$ 87.7	2.5	$ 183.4	1.2
Commerce	3.3	4.5	8.2	1.0	20.4	.6	84.5	.6
Defense	26.4	35.6	592.2	69.3	2,639.0	76.6	7,517.0	51.2
Health, Education, and Welfare	2.8	3.8	22.8	2.6	86.2	2.6	793.4	5.4
Interior	7.9	10.6	31.4	3.6	35.7	1.0	102.0	.7
Atomic Energy Commission			107.5	12.6	474.0	13.7	1,505.0	10.2
Federal Aviation Agency							74.0	.6
National Aeronautics and Space Administration[a]	2.2	3.0	37.5	4.4	71.1	2.1	4,171.0	28.4
National Science Foundation					15.4	.4	189.8	1.3
Veterans Administration					6.1	.2	34.1	.2
All other agencies	2.4	3.2	12.7	1.5	10.4	.3	39.7	.2
	74.1	100.0	854.7	100.0	3,446.0	100.0	14,693.9	100.0

SOURCE: Calculated from Edwin Mansfield, *The Economics of Technological Change* (New York: W. W. Norton and Company, Inc., 1968), Table 6.1, p. 163.
[a]National Advisory Committee on Aeronautics prior to 1958.

Europe, particularly important because it is financed to a much larger extent in the United States by the federal government.[17]

The relative magnitude of the flow of scientists and engineers to the United States from various countries reinforces these findings on the impact of federal government spending on the price of human capital. France has always been noted as having a very low flow of scientists and engineers to the United States. Brinley

TABLE 33.—FUNDS FOR RESEARCH AND DEVELOPMENT BY SOURCE IN VARIOUS COUNTRIES (IN PERCENTAGES)

COUNTRY	YEAR	GOVERNMENT	BUSINESS	NON-PROFIT SECTOR INCLUDING HIGHER EDUCATION	TOTAL
France	1961	78	22		100
United States	1961	66	32	2	100
Finland	1956	62	38		100
United Kingdom	1961	61	37	2	100
Canada	1959	61	31	8	100
Norway	1960	51	42	7	100
Japan	1959	36	64		100
Netherlands	1959	30	63	7	100

SOURCE: Mansfield, Table 6.10, p. 198.

Thomas has calculated the annual average immigration of S & E from selected countries to the United States from 1956 to 1961 as a percentage of the corresponding 1959 output of scientists and engineers of these countries. France had the lowest percentage figure, .9, while Germany's ratio was 8.2, the Netherlands' 15.1, the United Kingdom's 7.4, Sweden's 8.8, and Norway's 16.2.[18] Thomas also studied United States federal expenditures on R & D and the immigration of scientists and engineers to the United States for the period 1953–65 and found "a close relationship between the annual percentage rates of change in federal expenditure on Research & Development and in immigration of professional manpower."[19]

17. See *The American Challenge* (New York: Atheneum, 1968). Servan-Schreiber claims that in 1965 "the Americans devoted 3.61 per cent of their national product to research and development, as against 2.01 per cent for the Europeans" (p. 63).

18. "Modern Migration," in *The Brain Drain*, p. 34. Mexico, the third country that has been identified as having undergone a demand reversal in human capital, has also been cited as having a relatively small brain drain. See also Baldwin, "Brain Drain or Overflow?" p. 367.

19. "Modern Migration," pp. 42–44. Thomas made this observation on the basis of an inspection of the graphs of the respective variables.

Thomas explains this last finding by the fact that "The elasticity of supply of scientists and engineers in the short run is necessarily low because of the time it takes to train new ones. Over a longer period, e.g., the last 20 years, the elasticity of supply in the United States appears to have been lower than one would have expected and has accentuated the dynamic shortage. The raiding parties are busy in Britain and other countries partly because of the sluggish way in which the American market works" (p. 45).

The United States and France, both having attempted to develop strong and independent national defense postures, especially in comparison with the other non-Communist countries, have both encountered a shortage of high-level manpower relative to other countries. The demand reversal observed for Mexico also may have been caused by the Mexican government's successful encouragement of skill intensive manufacturing facilities. However, it was done with developmental planning rather than national defense planning. Public investment rose from 4 per cent of GNP in 1939–42 to about 5 per cent in 1959–60, including construction for manufacturing plants for steel, chemicals, transportation equipment, and petroleum refining.[20] More important, though, were a set of government policies that had the effect of redistributing income in favor of the upper income classes: "Specifically, protection, credit manipulation, and tax exemptions greatly enlarged investment yields without a corresponding rise in private saving. Earlier calculations of profits rising from 27 per cent of national income in 1939–40 to 41 per cent by 1950 appear exaggerated, but few informed observers doubt that incomes of owners and salaried professionals grew faster than wages" (p. 286). The result was that between 1940 and 1965, manufacturing output expanded 6.3-fold, and within the manufacturing sector the skill intensive industries, chemicals, machinery, and metal products, expanded their share of output from 17 to 38 per cent between 1950 and 1958 (pp. 285–86).

Generally, with industrialization, both the supply and demand of human capital can be expected to increase with, in most cases, supply increasing faster than demand. But this process can easily be upset as it was in the case of the United States, France, and

20. W. Paul Strassman, *Technological Change and Economic Development, the Manufacturing Experience of Mexico and Puerto Rico* (Ithaca: Cornell University Press, 1968), p. 287. Strassman chose Mexico for his case study because of its rapid rate of technological growth.

Mexico by strong autonomous increases in demand for human capital on the part of the national government.[21] In the case of the United States, the high price of human capital has evidently not interfered with her ability to export skill intensive products, but for France the evidence presented above indicates that the high price has prevented France from exporting these products. We do not have comparable trade data for Mexico.

The next question that arises is how these findings fit in with the various trade theories that were examined in chapters 1–3. For the United States, the Heckscher-Ohlin theory, even modified to bring in human capital, is not supported by the data except for natural resource influenced trade. Another explanation for the United States comparative advantage in skill intensive products must be sought. However, this theory does seem to be appropriate for the other countries in our sample, including France. Despite France's relative abundance of human capital on a quantity definition, which is just a little less than that of the United States,[22] her exports are not skill intensive. This is consistent with a properly specified factor endowments theory, since France has a relative scarcity of human capital on a price definition.[23] The factor abundance on both definitions in the other countries and their trade patterns are all consistent with the Heckscher-Ohlin model.

In chapters 2 and 3, the product cycle theory as proposed by Raymond Vernon was presented and tested for the United States. United States data at the two-digit industry level strongly supported the model. However, it was also pointed out that the Heckscher-Ohlin and product cycle models were not necessarily competing theories, but, indeed, fitted very nicely together, and that a synthesized model in certain cases performed significantly better than either model separately. Given that the Heckscher-Ohlin model as

21. A similar although less specific idea was expressed in 1956 by L. G. Reynolds and C. H. Taft, *The Evolution of Wage Structure* (New Haven: Yale University Press, 1956), p. 356: "One can thus argue that interindustry wage dispersion tends to reach a maximum some time during the early stages of industrialization and to diminish gradually after that point. The decline of differentials can be postponed, however, by a high rate of technical change, leading to rapid shifts of labor demand and continual churning up of new industries to the surface of the wage structure. The persistence of large differentials in countries like Canada and the United States can perhaps be rationalized on these grounds."

22. See Table 20.

23. Note, however, that this is a weaker form of the Heckscher-Ohlin theory. See the quote by Södersten, chap. 4n3.

tested in chapter 3 is inappropriate, considering the findings on factor abundance, we are then left with the need to explain the significant positive results of testing it. The model is based on the assumption that causality runs from factor endowments to trade patterns, but correlation analysis between factor endowment characteristics and trade pattern characteristics shows only association, not causality. Thus, given the refutation of a basic assumption of the Heckscher-Ohlin theory and the strong support for the product cycle theory which itself is based on the demand side, the causality could run from the trade patterns and the demand characteristics of a given country to the supply side or the endowment characteristics of that country. If a country has a strong propensity to develop new products endogenously through, say, a product cycle mechanism and also exogenously through a strong government demand, and if new product development is skill intensive, then it is possible that the country might have a physical abundance of human capital at the same time it has an economic shortage of it. This is exactly what we have observed for the United States. Finis Welch has attempted to answer the question "With the phenomenal rise in average education, why have rates of return failed to decline?"[24] He proposes several explanations that are similar to product cycle explanations: "As incomes rise, the composition of consumption changes; and if income elasticities of demand are positively related to the share of skilled labor among industries, the demand for skilled labor will rise relative to the demand for other forms of labor," and "Technical change may not be neutral between skill classes. It may be that increments in technology result in increments in the relative productivity of labor that are positively related to skill level" (pp. 37–38). Both explanations serve to increase endogenously the demand for skilled labor. The first is identical to the proposition put forth in chapter 2 to reconcile the differences between the product cycle and the Heckscher-Ohlin-Keesing theories. The second also may partly explain the demand reversal for human capital in the United States and is the one for which Welch provides empirical support.

Thus, if the endogenous and exogenous demands on skilled labor are strong enough, it may mean that factor endowments may not be the cause of trade but the result. This possibility has long been re-

24. "Education in Production," *Journal of Political Economy* 78 (January 1970): 36.

alized by Heckscher-Ohlin theorists. Indeed, even Ohlin pointed out that "the supply of industrial agents may sometimes more adequately be described as the *result* of trade than as its cause, although its being the outcome of an *earlier* economic situation does not prevent it from explaining and determining the nature of present trade."[25] This warning from Ohlin means that correlation analysis cannot be taken as unequivocal support for the factor endowments approach. Valavanis-Vail and Keesing also realized this possibility: "Even regarding the link between factors and trade, the Heckscher-Ohlin theory postulates unreal causal relationship. 'In the dynamic case, the producible factors of production, given time, adjust precisely to the pattern of final demand. It makes no sense to speak of "original endowments" unless one is speaking of the immediate short run.' In other words, a series of events largely unrelated to factor availabilities could have 'caused' observed patterns of location and trade, which in turn could have created factor supplies tailored to the factor requirements of the goods actually traded."[26]

This is exactly what has happened in the United States. Further, the "series of events largely unrelated to factor availabilities" that could have caused the observed patterns of trade and factor availability have been tentatively identified as the set of circumstances associated with the product cycle theory. However, several other factors could have acted in concert with the product cycle theory or alone and produced the same results. A full discussion of these other factors or theories is beyond the scope of this work but will be briefly discussed in an attempt to determine avenues for further research.

A major shortcoming of the product cycle theory is that it fails to emphasize the role of the United States government in adding to private demand for new products and technology. The product cycle model relies on the endogenous mechanism of the high per capita income and high labor costs in the United States in bringing about the development first in the United States of both income elastic new consumer goods and labor-saving new producer goods.

25. Bertil Ohlin, *Interregional and International Trade* (Cambridge: Harvard University Press, 1933), p. 67. Italics in the original as quoted by Caves, *Trade and Economic Structure*, p. 102.

26. Keesing, "Labor Skills and the Structure of Trade in Manufactures," in *The Open Economy*, pp. 2, 4. The quote within the quote is from Valavanis-Vail, "Leontief's Scarce Factor Paradox," p. 524.

The findings in this chapter indicate that we should add to this the new products and technology that the United States has developed because of the government's tremendous demand for highly complex weapons and space systems. This explanation can be brought easily into the product cycle framework.

Another way to look at the United States' government support of private research and development is as a government subsidy to a particular set of firms or industries.[27] This would then explain the comparative advantage these firms or industries enjoy. However, Keesing has attempted to examine the differential effects of company R & D and federal R & D. He wished to test the hypothesis that company R & D would have a greater impact on trade, dollar for dollar, than federal R & D, presumably because the products developed by private R & D would have a greater chance of being exported. Since this expectation is just the opposite of Kaliski's, it is not surprising that Keesing's evidence is inconclusive. The linear correlation between the company R & D variable and an index of United States export performance was less than the linear correlation between the federal R & D measure and export performance. However, these results were reversed when a rank correlation coefficient was calculated.[28] Thus, the two effects could be canceling each other out or both could be non-existent.

Another area in need of further research is the possibility of economies of scale to R & D, either internal or external to the firm. If there are economies of scale to R & D, then the United States would have a comparative advantage in the development of new products due simply to her large absolute number of scientists and engineers. In this case, whether the United States has a relatively large number of scientists and engineers or whether she has low relative wages for human capital would be of secondary importance in determining the United States' comparative advantage. Indeed, this would also explain why human capital does not appear to be the United States' relatively abundant factor on a price definition. Assuming competitive labor markets, the marginal product of skilled labor, and thus wage rates, would be absolutely and perhaps relatively higher in the United States due to the economies of scale in

27. This point was first brought out by S. F. Kaliski, "The R & D Factor in U.S. Trade—A Comment," *Journal of Political Economy* 75 (October 1967): 761–62.

28. Keesing, "The Impact of Research and Development on United States Trade," in *The Open Economy*, pp. 178, 179.

research and development. To the extent that this explanation has some validity, it contradicts the Heckscher-Ohlin theory, which assumes constant returns to scale and could be incorporated easily into the product cycle theory.[29] There is some empirical evidence of internal economies of scale to R & D in the chemical industry. Edwin Mansfield found that "when the size of the firm is held constant, the evidence seems to suggest that increases in R and D expenditures result in more than proportional increases in inventive output in the chemical industry. However, in petroleum and steel, there is no real indication that b is positive."[30] However, he also notes that "Most of the firms that are included here spent a reasonably large amount on R and D, generally several hundred thousands of dollars a year or more. There may be considerable economies of scale in the lower ranges of spending" (p. 42n).

In explaining the observed United States comparative advantage in R & D intensive industries, economies of scale external to the firm and the industry might also be important. This would be true if the rate of diffusion of new technology or products is discrete with regard to national boundaries. In other words the externalities first benefit the other firms and industries in the innovating country and then benefit the firms in the rest of the world. Kenneth Arrow stresses this point as an explanation of the "international inequalities in productivity," pointing out that the transmission of knowledge on the frontier is especially facilitated by personal contacts.[31] And in most cases, intra-country personal contacts will be greater than inter-country personal contacts.

Thus, it seems likely that there are economies of scale to R & D that are external within the United States but not without. Indeed, the observation that technical change historically has been accelerating in the United States is an indication of economies of scales

29. The phenomenon of economies of scale to R & D is not mentioned by Vernon, although economies of scale in general do play an important part in the product cycle theory. However, empirical investigations performed in chapter 3 did not reveal any significant association between export performance and two measures of economies of scale.

30. *Industrial Research and Technological Innovation* (New York: W. W. Norton and Company, Inc., 1968), p. 42. The letter b is the coefficient of R & D squared, so that a positive coefficient shows that economies of scale are present while a negative coefficient would show that diseconomies of scale were present. For steel and petroleum no diseconomies of scale were found.

31. "Classificatory Notes on the Production and Transmission of Technological Knowledge," *American Economic Review, Papers and Proceedings* 59 (May 1969): 32–34.

to R & D.[32] The fact that the rate of productivity growth in other countries has been faster recently than in the United States is not inconsistent with this hypothesis, since innovating new products and imitating them are different processes. Both of these hypotheses fit very well into the product cycle theory since Vernon emphasizes the importance of communication and external economies, although not specifically with regard to R & D.[33] Thus, further research is needed especially with regard to various types of economies of scale to R & D and the rate of diffusion of technology. This is particularly true in light of our findings on demand reversals and the fact that economies of scale to R & D could help explain this phenomenon.

Another factor which might explain the United States' superiority in skill intensive products, given the relatively higher wage rates for skilled labor in the United States, relies, as did the economies of scale argument, on relatively higher productivities of skilled labor in the United States than in the rest of the world. Of course, this approach also violates the Heckscher-Ohlin assumption of perfect competition which results in wage rates equal to the value marginal product of labor. In light of the evidence in the earlier part of this chapter on the post–World War II labor market for scientists and engineers, it seems probable that a dynamic shortage was characteristic of this period. Indeed, this was the conclusion of Arrow and Capron as well as Hansen in their studies of this labor market, and of Brinley Thomas in his examination of the reasons for the brain drain.[34] A "dynamic shortage" results when the demand curve steadily shifts rightward and the quantity supplied does not instantaneously adjust to each shift.[35] Obviously in the labor market which is not perfectly competitive, wages do not adjust instantaneously to

32. See Robert M. Solow, "Technical Change and the Aggregate Production Function," *Review of Economics and Statistics* 39 (August 1957): 312–20. However, Arrow does not believe that this can continue: "But of course exponential technological growth does have the advantage of being consistent with observed facts: If anything, the observed rate of growth of total factor productivity is increasing. I can only conjecture that, as in the case of population, the true law is something like the logistic curve, but we are still in the early phases, which resemble the exponential" (p. 34).

33. See Vernon, "International Investment and International Trade in the Product Cycle," pp. 194–96.

34. See Arrow and Capron, p. 302; Hansen, p. 212; and Thomas, pp. 43–44.

35. Arrow and Capron were the first to use this term in this context (p. 301).

shifts in the demand and supply curves. Arrow and Capron argue that wages adjust even more slowly in the market for scientific personnel than in most labor markets due to the prevalence of long-term contracts, the heterogeneity of the market which slows information, and the dominance of a relatively small number of firms in R & D who act as oligopsonists with no raiding agreements.[36] In addition, the more rapid increase in demand and the inelastic supply due to long training periods increase the shortage.

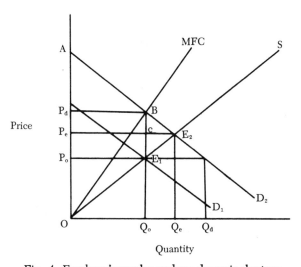

Fig. 4. Employer's surplus under a dynamic shortage

For our purposes the significance of this dynamic shortage of scientists and engineers is that firms will be paying their scientists and engineers wages that are below their marginal revenue product. This point is illustrated in Figure 4 which shows the labor market for scientists and engineers. The demand curve is continually shifting to the right and, therefore, a dynamic shortage exists. This is illustrated in Figure 4 by the comparative statics approach of shifting the demand curve from D_1 to D_2 and assuming that the price stays at P_o.[37] A dynamic shortage exists because the quantity demand, Q_d, is greater than the quantity supplied, Q_o. In addition, the marginal revenue product of the last worker hired and, therefore, the demand price, P_d, is greater than the supply price, P_o. Under very plausible assumptions this will mean an increase in profits to the firms hiring scientists and engineers. The gain to the firms can be calculated by comparing the areas under the marginal revenue product curves, i.e., the demand curves, minus the total wage bill for the case of the dynamic shortage (area ABE_1P_0 in Figure 4) with the same measure for the equilibrium case (area AE_2P_e). The net gain in profits is, therefore, equal to

$$(1) \qquad (P_e - P_o) \, Q_o - \frac{1}{2}(Q_e - Q_o) \, (P_d - P_e)$$

where P_0 and Q_0 are the actual wage rate and number of workers employed, P_e and Q_e are the wage rate and quantity employed that would prevail if there were no dynamic shortage, and P_d equals the demand price or the marginal revenue product of the last worker hired.

Thus, the more inelastic the supply curve and, therefore, the greater P_e, and the more elastic the demand curve and, therefore, the less P_d, the greater would be the possible gain in profits to the firms employing scientists and engineers. It is possible for the dynamic shortage to lead to a net loss of profits if the equilibrium quantity is very large relative to the actual quantity employed and if supply is elastic and demand inelastic. However, this is quite unlikely since the supply curve is probably inelastic and since the additional scientists and engineers that would be hired at equilibrium $(Q_e - Q_0)$ would probably not approach the original number already hired, Q_0.[38] Note that wages are rising but not fast enough to clear the market since the demand curve is continually shifting to the right.

Another method of showing the gain to firms that employ scientists and engineers, given a dynamic shortage, is to draw in the

---

and for proof of the assertion that the actual price will always remain below the equilibrium price as long as demand is increasing.

38. For example, if we assume that the supply and demand curves have the same absolute slopes, then the vacancy rate (dynamic shortage) has to be four times the number of scientists and engineers currently employed for the dynamic shortage to lead to a fall in profits. To show this, solve: (1) setting $P_e - P_0 = P_d - P_e$ since the absolute slopes are the same. Thus, $Q_e = 3Q_0$ and substituting $3Q_0$ for $Q_e - Q_0$ gives the value $2Q_0$. To get the vacancy rate $Q_d - Q_e$, we can double $2Q_0$ due to the equal absolute slopes assumption.

marginal factor cost curve illustrating the profit-maximizing input price and the resulting marginal revenue product if these firms acted as a single monopsonist. If the input price under the dynamic shortage case and the factor price under the monopsonist assumption case were the same, then the dynamic shortage case would by chance have maximized the profits earned from the S & E inputs of these firms. This has been done in Figure 4.

Thus, the assumptions necessary for this explanation to be valid are that there exists in the United States a dynamic shortage in the market for skilled labor but not in the market for unskilled labor, and that this situation does not exist in the rest of the world. Further, it is necessary that the United States enjoy a comparative advantage in skilled labor intensive products before the creation of the dynamic shortage in the United States by the large autonomous government demand for research and development. If this were not the case, the increase in demand for R & D would drive the price up in the United States; and even though this would create a dynamic shortage of scientists and engineers and an increase in profits for scientists and engineering intensive firms, the higher product price would prevent the United States from exporting this type of good. However, if the United States already had a comparative advantage in skilled labor intensive products, the increase in government demand for these products would not be as likely to price these products out of world markets as if there were a dynamic shortage which allowed firms to reap bonuses from their skilled labor or pass on this saving in the form of lower prices. Thus, this factor may have allowed the United States to maintain a comparative advantage in skill intensive products longer than she would have in the face of a strong increase in domestic demand for these products. And this comparative advantage was maintained by firms paying a factor input less than its marginal revenue product.

Finally, the effect of the brain drain itself on United States comparative advantage should be examined further.[39] The actual flow

39. There have been a few studies on the effect of the brain drain on the composition of the stock of United States skilled labor but none relating it to United States comparative advantage. See Herbert Grubel, "Foreign Manpower in the U.S. Sciences," *Income and Wealth* (March 1968), pp. 57–74. Grubel estimates that 11.5 per cent of all United States scientists with Ph.D.'s are of foreign origin. See also Grubel and Anthony Scott, "The Immigration of Scientists and Engineers to the United States, 1949–61," *Journal of Political Economy* 74, no. 4 (August 1966): 368–78.

of scientists and engineers should strengthen the Heckscher-Ohlin mechanisms since it would tend to increase both the physical and economic abundance of human capital in the United States and decrease it in the rest of the world. Also it tends to increase the elasticity of supply of scientists and engineers and reduce the strength of the dynamic shortage mechanism of comparative advantage, already mentioned. So far, however, the migration of scientists and engineers evidently has not had this effect; the brain drain can be looked at as a symptom of these factors, but a symptom that tends to be partially offsetting. The brain drain could be building a basis for a United States comparative advantage in human capital along Heckscher-Ohlin grounds in the future, which then could either replace or complement the product cycle theory as discussed in chapter 2.

Apparently, the empirical support for the Heckscher-Ohlin theory, the product cycle theory, and the synthesis of the two theories found in chapters 1–3, on the one hand, and the findings on the different definitions of factor abundance in chapter 4, on the other, can be reconciled by the strong endogenous demand for human capital encompassed by the product cycle and by the strong autonomous demand for human capital as a result of our national defense and space policies.[40] Given the findings on factor abundance, the high correlation between measures of factor intensity and export performance is consistent with the view that factor endowments follow from demand conditions and trade patterns, rather than cause them. The United States' comparative advantage in skill intensive products must be due to mechanisms such as the product cycle model, the government subsidy of R & D explanation, the economies of scale in R & D arguments, or the dynamic shortage theory.

40. Note that the recent "loosening supply-and-demand situation among R & D scientists and engineers" has been directly attributed by the U.S. Department of Labor to "the leveling off in Government expenditures for research and development" (see Department of Labor, *Manpower Report of the President*, p. 167). This development lends support to an explanation which emphasizes the importance of exogenous influences in the market for skilled labor.

6. The Future Role of the United States in International Trade

This study has examined closely the two major theories purporting to explain United States trade patterns in manufactures: the Heckscher-Ohlin theory, modified to bring in human capital, and the product cycle theory. Both have appeared in their current versions in the last few years and have been hailed by their supporters as major advancements in the theory of international trade. As stated, they differ in their explanation of the same phenomena, presenting enough conflict to warrant an investigation of their empirical validity in an effort to reconcile their differences. After critical examination of both theoretical antecedents and empirical support, it has been concluded, with a few qualifications and modifications, that both theories are indeed sound, and, moreover, that both explain United States trade patterns in manufactures quite well. Thus, a reconciliation of these findings was needed; it was observed that theoretically the two approaches could be made consistent with and complementary to each other. Indeed, there are good theoretical reasons for doing so, since the Heckscher-Ohlin theory is mainly a static one based on the supply side and the product cycle theory a more dynamic one that stresses the demand side. A simple model combining features of both models was proposed and tested empirically.

Although the statistical results were mixed, on the whole they supported the technology based product cycle approach. In addition, consideration of the United States' actual relative "economic" abundance of human capital vis-à-vis its main trading partners lent further support to the product cycle theory. Although physical abundance is obvious, it does not appear that the United States can also claim an "economic" abundance of human capital. Therefore, the factor proportions approach cannot logically explain the observed United States trade patterns in manufactures. The explanation for the demand reversal was found to rely upon the tremendous increase in governmental demand associated with the rise of the military industrial complex in the fifties and early sixties; this apparently bid up the relative price of United States skilled manpower above that observed in our major trading partners.

The product cycle dominance may be only temporary and probably does not explain the trade flows of other countries as well as it does those of the United States. In the long run, economists expect both supply and demand to be important. In fact, developments in the United States in the late sixties and early seventies already seem to indicate a revival of the importance of the supply side.

The recent cutback in governmental support of R & D, the slowing down of the brain drain, and the hard times that the high technology industries have recently experienced have coincided with the deterioration of United States international competitiveness. The high cost of skilled manpower in the United States is becoming a disadvantage as the product cycle forces weaken. The harmful employment effects on United States skilled manpower are particularly harsh consequences of this process.

If the United States desires to maintain its comparative advantage in high technology products, either skill differentials must fall or basic research and development efforts must increase. The government can encourage both by continued aid to higher education, thus maintaining the United States' lead in physical human capital abundance, by holding skill differentials down, and by stepping up subsidization of research and development, especially in the nondefense and space industries, which up to now have been relatively neglected.

These arguments in favor of aid to education and subsidization of research and development are fundamentally different from the usual arguments made in support of these government services (i.e., the public good and externality arguments), because they are predicated on the assumption that the United States should attempt to maintain a comparative advantage in high technology products. This may or may not be desirable on the grounds of strict economic efficiency. However, to the extent that there are externalities associated with high technology or human capital intensive industries, such government policy can be recommended on economic grounds.

Appendix

TABLE 34.—INDICES OF EXPORT PERFORMANCE

SIC #	1958		1960		1965		1966	
	X₁ (millions)	X₂ (%)	X₁ (millions)	X₂ (%)	X₁ (millions)	X₂ (%)	X₁ (millions)	X₂ (%)
20	–297	–.5	–256	–.4	80	.1	–439	–.6
21	80	2.1	92	2.0	118	2.5	123	2.6
22	–102	–.8	–300	–2.0	–473	–2.6	–541	–2.8
23	–55	–.4	–155	–.9	–364	–2.0	–413	–2.1
24	–302	–4.0	–350	–4.2	–408	–4.0	–437	–4.1
25	23	.5	12	.2	–17	–.3	–39	–.5
26	–641	–5.0	–636	–4.1	–658	–3.6	–729	–3.6
27	82	.7	100	.6	153	.8	170	.8
28	1,229	5.3	1,667	5.7	1,960	5.3	2,058	5.0
29	–151	–1.0	–174	–1.0	–486	–2.6	–523	–2.6
30	121	1.8	35	.4	74	.7	62	.5
31	–46	–1.2	–79	–1.8	–196	–4.2	–240	–4.8
32	23	.2	–32	–.3	15	.1	–18	–.1
33	–49	–.2	–177	–.5	–1,341	–3.0	–1,795	–3.6
34	464	2.4	306	1.4	541	2.0	672	2.2
35	2,404	10.5	2,703	9.6	4,015	10.2	3,913	8.4
36	825	4.2	724	2.6	765	2.2	643	1.6
37	1,848	4.8	2,008	3.9	2,010	3.0	1,356	1.9
38	192	4.3	221	3.3	408	5.4	485	5.5
39	–123	–2.5	–191	–1.8	–239	–3.2	–289	–3.6

SOURCES: The X₁s have been calculated by subtracting imports from exports. The data are from various issues of *U.S. Commodity Exports and Imports as Related to Output*. The X₂'s are the X₁'s divided by shipments. Shipments have been taken from various issues of the *Annual Survey of Manufactures*.

TABLE 35.—FACTOR INTENSITY VARIABLES FOR 1960

	N–W&S (dollars)	W&S (dollars)	L–S (per cent)	M	C (per cent)
20	6,700	4,780	2.48	10.4	.78
21	14,860	3,870	2.18	9.5	.49
22	2,740	3,570	1.90	8.7	.41
23	2,110	3,130	1.10	10.1	.41
24	3,210	3,640	1.27	8.6	.37
25	2,990	4,200	1.96	9.4	.49
26	8,930	5,380	5.07	10.8	1.35
27	4,620	5,580	9.16	11.6	2.17
28	13,790	6,120	15.65	12.2	5.28
29	13,230	6,690	15.07	12.3	4.51
30	4,690	5,280	5.79	11.2	1.82
31	2,280	3,570	.87	9.1	.39
32	5,720	5,050	4.96	9.9	1.19
33	5,160	6,140	5.60	10.1	1.17
34	4,330	5,150	9.66	11.2	1.92
35	4,170	5,930	9.38	11.6	1.60
36	4,360	5,390	15.23	12.3	3.19
37	5,040	6,510	12.19	11.5	2.20
38	5,350	5,920	16.18	12.3	3.67
39	3,640	5,330	3.27	10.7	1.03

SOURCES: N–W&S and W&S are value added minus wages and salary divided by total employees for each industry and wages and salary divided by total employment, respectively. The data are from the *Annual Survey of Manufactures, 1959 and 1960*, and the calculations are the author's. L–S is the ratio of professional, technical, and kindred workers to total employment and was calculated by David Ball from the U.S. *Census of Population: 1960*, "Occupation by Industry." M and C are the median school years completed by males and the percentage of workers having completed five years of college to total workers for each industry, respectively. These indices were computed by the author from U.S. *Census of Population: 1960*, "Industrial Characteristics," PC(2)–7F.

TABLE 36.—INDICES OF LABOR SKILLS FOR 1950, 1960, AND 1965

	1950 (per cent)	1960 (per cent)	1965 (per cent)
20	2.61	2.48	2.4
21	1.07	2.18	3.4
22	1.41	1.90	2.2
23	1.04	1.10	1.1
24	.86	1.27	1.5
25	1.61	1.96	2.2
26	3.39	5.07	6.3
27	9.51	9.16	9.0
28	11.78	15.65	13.2
29	14.00	15.07	15.7
30	5.38	5.79	6.0
31	.95	.87	.8
32	4.04	4.96	5.7
33	4.08	5.60	6.7
34	4.75	9.66	14.7
35	6.76	9.38	11.3
36	9.24	15.23	20.1
37	6.60	12.19	17.3
38	9.29	16.18	22.2
39	3.14	3.27	3.3

SOURCES: The skill index for 1950 was computed by the author from Occupation by Industry of the *U.S. Census of Population: 1950,* vol. 4, part 1, chapter C, Table 2. It is the percentage of professional, technical, and kindred workers to total employment in each industry. The skill index for 1960 was computed by David Ball using the 1960 census data and the same method as above. The skill index for 1965 was computed by the formula

$$L\text{-}S_{65} = \frac{1}{2}\left[\frac{L\text{-}S_{60}}{L\text{-}S_{50}} - 1\right] + L\text{-}S_{60}.$$

This formula simply extrapolates the trend from 1950 to 1960 on to 1965.

TABLE 37.—INDICES OF TOTAL, PHYSICAL, AND HUMAN CAPITAL INTENSITY
FOR 1958, 1965, AND 1966

	1958			1965			1966		
	VA/L	N–W&S	W&S	VA/L	N–W&S	W&S	VA/L	N–W&S	W&S
20	$10,321	$ 5,875	$4,446	109	124	91	$15,162	$ 9,351	$5,811
21	16,728	13,237	3,492	179	269	77	25,870	20,947	4,923
22	5,387	2,129	3,258	64	57	72	8,657	4,082	2,575
23	5,085	2,048	3,037	49	39	61	6,779	2,972	2,807
24	5,465	2,049	3,416	59	46	73	8,405	3,687	4,718
25	6,758	2,762	3,996	68	56	81	9,292	4,186	5,106
26	10,275	5,234	5,041	105	107	104	14,856	8,175	6,681
27	9,169	3,984	5,185	94	85	104	13,035	6,403	6,632
28	17,549	11,651	5,898	193	260	117	27,735	20,282	7,453
29	14,054	8,820	6,234	220	303	126	33,643	25,632	8,011
30	9,419	4,465	4,954	93	88	99	12,763	6,517	6,246
31	5,434	2,151	3,283	53	42	66	7,274	3,093	4,181
32	9,980	5,296	4,684	101	104	97	13,733	7,529	6,204
33	10,646	4,897	5,749	115	110	121	16,120	8,476	7,644
34	8,897	3,782	5,115	93	84	103	12,613	6,028	6,585
35	9,191	3,774	5,417	105	95	116	14,989	7,522	7,476
36	9,263	4,267	4,996	96	88	105	12,977	6,367	6,610
37	9,811	3,928	5,883	122	116	128	15,476	7,301	8,175
38	9,798	4,477	5,321	117	124	110	16,124	9,170	6,954
39	8,312	3,329	4,983	81	32	81	10,437	5,354	5,143

SOURCES: The 1958 indices were computed by the author from *1958 Census of Manufactures*, vol. I, Table 3. VA/L is value added divided by total employment, W&S is payroll divided by total employment, and N–W&S is value added minus payroll divided by total employment. The 1965 indices are from Lary's *Imports of Manufactures from Less Developed Countries*, Table 2, and were computed as above except that Lary's index is in the form of percentage of national average. The 1966 indices were computed by the author in the same way as the 1958 indices. The 1966 indices are based on the *Annual Survey of Manufactures, 1966*.

TABLE 38.—MATRIX OF SIMPLE CORRELATION COEFFICIENTS IN THE TEST OF THE HECKSCHER-OHLIN MODEL, 1960

X_1					
.911**	X_2				
.528*	.589**	L–S			
.403	.469*	.937**	C		
.466*	.471*	.800**	.745**	W&S	
.070	.190	.364	.522*	.361	N–W&S

*Indicates significance at the .05 level.
**Indicates significance at the .01 level.

TABLE 39.—MATRIX OF SIMPLE CORRELATION COEFFICIENTS IN THE TEST OF THE HECKSCHER-OHLIN MODEL, 1965

X_1					
.875**	X_2				
.482*	.608**	L–S			
.416	.479*	.718**	W&S		
.129	.263	.407	.469*	N–W&S	
–.391	–.355	–.053	.349	.320	D

*Indicates significance at the .05 level.
**Indicates significance at the .01 level.

TABLE 40.—PRODUCT CYCLE VARIABLES

	S&E (per cent)	VA (per cent)	L–C	O/S	ES₁ ($1,000)	ES₂
20	.3	259	.0045	.81	240	140
21	.2	277	.0633	.70	15,278	400
22	.3	140	.0047	.83	752	58
23	.1	190	.0060	.80	156	55
24	.1	176	.0585	.82	69	145
25	.2	263	.0113	.78	132	105
26	.3	292	−.0038	.76	503	141
27	.2	278	−.0023	.70	112	123
28	4.1	388	.0111	.61	447	158
29	1.8	206	−.0267	.86	1,096	98
30	.5	434	−.0028	.75	227	125
31	.1	152	−.0045	.80	379	75
32	.1	344	.0232	.69	146	126
33	.5	325	−.0553	.79	885	142
34	.4	289	−.0377	.77	182	112
35	1.4	292	.0299	.75	232	106
36	3.6	519	−.0346	.74	391	118
37	3.4	487	.0075	.80	816	129
38	3.4	467	.0060	.67	274	126
39	.3	193	−.1400	.74	142	126

SOURCES: S&E is the percentage of scientists and engineers engaged in research and development to the total labor force. This has been computed by Gruber et al. for 1962, except for SIC 39 which has been computed by the author from the *1963 Census of Manufactures*. VA is the 1965 value added divided by 1947 value added which was computed by the author from the *Annual Survey of Manufactures, 1949 and 1950* and from *Annual Survey of Manufactures, 1965*. L–C is the rate of growth of labor efficiency minus the rate of growth of capital efficiency which was estimated for 1948 to 1962 by Ferguson and Moroney in "Sources of Change in Labor's Relative Share: A Neoclassical Analysis." O/S is cost of materials plus payroll divided by shipments and is provided for 1963 in the *1963 Census of Manufactures*. ES₁ is the value added per establishment for 1963 and has been calculated by the author from the *1963 Census of Manufactures*. ES₂ is the value added per laborer for establishments with over 250 employees to value added per employee for establishments with under ten employees and has been calculated by the writer from R. Nelson, "International Productivity Differences," *American Economic Review* 58 (December 1968): 1240.

TABLE 41.—1965 MATRIX OF SIMPLE LINEAR CORRELATION COEFFICIENTS FOR THE PRODUCT CYCLE VARIABLES

X_1					
.875**	X_2				
.396	.577*	VA			
.533*	.573**	.722**	S&E		
−.344	−.560**	−.501*	−.390	O/S	
.250	.298	.028	−.017	−.088	L–C

*Indicates significance at the .05 level.
**Indicates significance at the .01 level.

TABLE 42.—MATRIX OF SIMPLE CORRELATION COEFFICIENTS FOR COMBINED FACTOR INTENSITY AND PRODUCT CYCLE VARIABLES

X_2								
.608**	L–S							
.479*	.778**	W&S						
.263	.407	.469*	N–W&S					
−.355	−.053	.349	.320	D				
.577**	.735**	.705**	.425*	−.128	VA			
.573**	.870**	.628**	.404	−.117	.722**	S&E		
−.560**	−.386	(−.210)	(−.278)	.391	−.501*	−.390	O/S	
.298	−.101	−.145	.047	−.193	.028	−.017	−.088	LC

*Indicates significance at the .05 level.
**Indicates significance at the .01 level.

TABLE 43.—MATRIX OF SIMPLE CORRELATION COEFFICIENTS FOR THE NINETEEN-INDUSTRY CASE

X_2								
.705**	L–S							
.445*	.780**	W&S						
.383	.415	(.464)*	N–W&S					
−.365	−.043	.387	.316	D				
.747**	.740**	.658**	(.425)	−.130	VA			
.687**	.885**	.632**	(.404)	−.117	.725**	S&E		
−.689**	−.384	−.210	(−.278)	.390	−.501*	−.388	O/S	
.236	−.121	−.194	(.047)	−.176	.030	−.028	−.083	L–C

*Indicates significance at the .05 level.
**Indicates significance at the .01 level.
( )Indicates the coefficient is for the twenty-industry case.

UNIVERSITY OF FLORIDA MONOGRAPHS

Social Sciences

1. *The Whigs of Florida, 1845–1854,* by Herbert J. Doherty, Jr.

2. *Austrian Catholics and the Social Question, 1918–1933,* by Alfred Diamant

3. *The Siege of St. Augustine in 1702,* by Charles W. Arnade

4. *New Light on Early and Medieval Japanese Historiography,* by John A. Harrison

5. *The Swiss Press and Foreign Affairs in World War II,* by Frederick H. Hartmann

6. *The American Militia: Decade of Decision, 1789–1800,* by John K. Mahon

7. *The Foundation of Jacques Maritain's Political Philosophy,* by Hwa Yol Jung

8. *Latin American Population Studies,* by T. Lynn Smith

9. *Jacksonian Democracy on the Florida Frontier,* by Arthur W. Thompson

10. *Holman Versus Hughes: Extension of Australian Commonwealth Powers,* by Conrad Joyner

11. *Welfare Economics and Subsidy Programs,* by Milton Z. Kafoglis

12. *Tribune of the Slavophiles: Konstantin Aksakov,* by Edward Chmielewski

13. *City Managers in Politics: An Analysis of Manager Tenure and Termination,* by Gladys M. Kammerer, Charles D. Farris, John M. DeGrove, and Alfred B. Clubok

14. *Recent Southern Economic Development as Revealed by the Changing Structure of Employment,* by Edgar S. Dunn, Jr.

15. *Sea Power and Chilean Independence,* by Donald E. Worcester

16. *The Sherman Antitrust Act and Foreign Trade,* by Andre Simmons

17. *The Origins of Hamilton's Fiscal Policies,* by Donald F. Swanson

18. *Criminal Asylum in Anglo-Saxon Law,* by Charles H. Riggs, Jr.

19. *Colonia Barón Hirsch, A Jewish Agricultural Colony in Argentina,* by Morton D. Winsberg

20. *Time Deposits in Present-Day Commercial Banking,* by Lawrence L. Crum

21. *The Eastern Greenland Case in Historical Perspective,* by Oscar Svarlien

22. *Jacksonian Democracy and the Historians,* by Alfred A. Cave

23. *The Rise of the American Chemistry Profession, 1850–1900,* by Edward H. Beardsley

24. *Aymara Communities and the Bolivian Agrarian Reform,* by William E. Carter

25. *Conservatives in the Progressive Era: The Taft Republicans of 1912,* by Norman M. Wilensky

26. *The Anglo-Norwegian Fisheries Case of 1951 and the Changing Law of the Territorial Sea,* by Teruo Kobayashi

27. *The Liquidity Structure of Firms and Monetary Economics,* by William J. Frazer, Jr.

28. *Russo-Persian Commercial Relations, 1828–1914,* by Marvin L. Entner

29. *The Imperial Policy of Sir Robert Borden,* by Harold A. Wilson

30. *The Association of Income and Educational Achievement,* by Roy L. Lassiter, Jr.

31. *Relation of the People to the Land in Southern Iraq,* by Fuad Baali

32. *The Price Theory of Value in Public Finance,* by Donald R. Escarraz

33. *The Process of Rural Development in Latin America,* by T. Lynn Smith

34. *To Be or Not to Be . . . Existential-Psychological Perspectives on the Self,* edited by Sidney M. Jourard

35. *Politics in a Mexican Community,* by Lawrence S. Graham

36. *A Two-Sector Model of Economic Growth with Technological Progress,* by Frederick Owen Goddard

37. *Florida Studies in the Helping Professions,* by Arthur W. Combs

38. *The Ancient Synagogues of the Iberian Peninsula,* by Don A. Halperin

39. *An Estimate of Personal Wealth in Oklahoma in 1960,* by Richard Edward French

40. *Congressional Oversight of Executive Agencies,* by Thomas A. Henderson

41. *Historians and Meiji Statesmen,* by Richard T. Chang

42. *Welfare Economics and Peak Load Pricing: A Theoretical Application to Municipal Water Utility Practices,* by Robert Lee Greene

43. *Factor Analysis in International Relations: Interpretation, Problem Areas, and an Application,* by Jack E. Vincent

44. *The Sorcerer's Apprentice: The French Scientist's Image of German Science, 1840–1919,* by Harry W. Paul

45. *Community Power Structure: Propositional Inventory, Tests, and Theory,* by Claire W. Gilbert

46. *Human Capital, Technology, and the Role of the United States in International Trade,* by John F. Morrall III

UNIVERSITY OF FLORIDA PRE
GAINESVILLE
1972